# RELEASING THE

# FORCE

## OF FAITH DECREES

## DESTINY IMAGE BOOKS AND COMPILATIONS BY LARRY SPARKS

# RELEASING THE
# FORCE
## OF FAITH DECREES

*Speaking Words that Carry the Spirit and Life of Jesus*

## LARRY SPARKS

DESTINY IMAGE® PUBLISHERS, INC.
P.O. Box 310, Shippensburg, PA 17257-0310
*"Publishing cutting-edge prophetic resources to supernaturally empower the body of Christ"*

This book and all other Destiny Image and Destiny Image Fiction books are available at Christian bookstores and distributors worldwide.

For more information on foreign distributors, call 717-532-3040.

Reach us on the Internet: www.destinyimage.com.

ISBN 13 TP: 978-0-7684-7261-5

ISBN 13 eBook: 978-0-7684-7262-2

ISBN 13 HC: 978-0-7684-7264-6

ISBN 13 LP: 978-0-7684-7263-9

For Worldwide Distribution, Printed in the U.S.A.

1 2 3 4 5 6 7 8 / 27 26 25 24 23

# CONTENTS

# INTRODUCTION

E very May 4 at Destiny Image, we recognize a new and increasingly iconic day of remembrance: *May the 4th.* Another read and you may get it: ***May the Fourth*** (like the Force) *Be with You.* Okay, so we are a publishing house filled with science fiction fans, like *Star Wars* (personally, I am a major fan of the original series: *New Hope* through *Return of the Jedi* and *Doctor Who*...namely, classic *Dr. Who,* but he has nothing to do with *May the 4th).* So, how does this at all relate to our mandate to steward timely and powerful prophetic words?

When decreed, the ***right words*** *have a supernatural force.* Both of our imprints, Destiny Image and Harrison House, carry multiple books by trusted ministry leaders writing about the supernatural power of your words. From faith classics by Charles Capps (*The Tongue: A Creative Force* and *Authority in Three Worlds)* to modern bestsellers including Brenda Kunneman's *The Daily Decree,* Jennifer LeClaire's *Victory Decrees,* and Tommy and Miriam Evans', *Decrees that Unlock Heaven's Power,* I pay attention when the Spirit of the Lord seems to be highlighting a certain topic (and multiple books are written and published on that subject).

We do *not* specifically go out of our way to find new decrees books—especially, lining up a whole bunch over a 1-2 year period. It happens organically, as I believe God is reminding us of how powerful the *right* words are. So I want to give you a Scripture that people do *not* tend to focus on when speaking of *decree, confession,* or *the power of words.* And yet, this might be the most powerful and foundational verse to give a context for *why* we believe in the power of speaking anointed words and making bold decrees.

In John 6:63, Jesus says, *"The words that I speak to you are spirit, and they are life."* This is why it's vital to be armed and equipped with Bible-based, Holy Spirit-anointed decrees: when you speak what God is saying, you will *see* what God says come to pass. Bottom line: When we say what Jesus would say, those words actually become a supernatural substance. They become spirit and life. But the key is speaking what *He* would say.

We don't have the right to go around "declaring and decreeing" any old thing we want, need, or desire. God is not our butler or a supernatural Santa Claus. But when we come into agreement with what God says and put *His words* in our mouths, I repeat, we will start to *see* what God said.

So I offer you *The Force of Faith Decrees* and encourage you: do *not* discount the force of your words. Life and death are in the power of the tongue (see Proverbs 18:21). This is why we offer this dynamic compilation to you, as these authors have done the heavy lifting, study, and hard work to bring you solid, sound, and supernatural Bible-based decrees that will equip you to hit the target when you pray.

# 1

# UNWRAP YOUR GIFT

by

*Larry Sparks*

*For it is by grace you have been saved, through
faith—and this is not from yourselves, it is
the gift of God* (Ephesians 2:8 NIV).

This faith to move mountains and supernaturally transform every impossible situation that comes against us is not out of our reach. It's not some upgraded version of faith reserved for the spiritually elite. Are you a Christian? If so, then this means you have *already received* breakthrough faith. It was God's gift to you, to both save you eternally and empower you to live victoriously while upon the earth.[1]

If we are believers in Christ, it is not necessary for us to run around, trying to get faith as if it's something we don't already possess. Rather, it is more like unwrapping a gift that we have already received. At the moment of our salvation, we received the key that transforms hope into reality, possibilities into solutions, and God's Word into life-changing supernatural power. And that key is faith. It's one of the most frequently preached about and written about topics in Christianity today—but do we really understand what faith is and how to use it to walk out a life-style of supernatural breakthrough?

In the pages ahead my goal is simple: I want to help you be aware of what you have already received at the moment of salvation and show you how to put it to work in your everyday life. The faith you received is not wimpy. It's not watered down. It's not some junior faith that is in need of a constant upgrade. You received supernatural faith from a supernatural God the moment you were born again.

Together we will navigate through some false understandings and doctrines about faith, press through the deceptions, and then learn how to put the truth into action. I share my up-and-down story with under-standing and activating faith, as I experienced *extremes* on both ends of the spectrum. Now, by God's grace, I am moving toward a healthy, Bible-based balance of what faith looks like and how it functions. My vision is to stir up the breakthrough faith inside you—faith that perse-veres through every obstacle and obtains the promises of God.

Throughout this journey together, we will establish solid, Scrip-ture-based foundations on what faith is and how to put it to work in our lives. This is why the book is broken up into two sections: Under-standing Faith and Activating Faith. Many books about faith focus on either understanding faith or activating faith, but I believe that in order to activate faith we need to have a solid, biblical understanding of what it actually is, where it comes from, and what it does. For faith principles to work effectively, they must be built on the pillar of the knowledge of God. Otherwise, at the first sign of resistance, we will break.

There are three groups of believers: The first group consists of those who have been striving to diligently work all of the faith principles, but after days, weeks, and even years of confessing, declaring, rebuking, reading, listening, and praying, they feel burned out and spiritually bankrupt. Hold on tight, friend. I believe the Holy Spirit is going to bring you some much-needed encouragement and balance.

The second group is those who need to learn about certain scriptural realities that they have never been exposed to before. In order for them to experience breakthrough, they need to be introduced to some new, and perhaps unusual, ways that God moves. To many, these realities include supernatural healing, deliverance, freedom from oppression, and restoration—to name just a few of the more popular topics. I am so excited to share these keys with you, keys that are going to birth within you a hunger to experience God's power in fresh, new, Bible-based ways.

> At the moment of our salvation, we received the key that transforms hope into reality, possibilities into solutions, and God's Word into life-changing supernatural power.

The third group is those who are hungry to experience *more* in their relationship with God. They are not content with a miracle on Sunday and a meltdown on Monday; they are pressing into a lifestyle of sustained, supernatural breakthrough. This desire burns in their hearts—and it should burn in the heart of every believer, for we were made for it. Christianity, in its current shape and form, does not satisfy them. There is a resounding cry from deep inside their spirit, telling them that there is a "new normal" available.

## Two Types of Faith

There are two types of faith believers tend to gravitate toward. First, we can fall prey to *experiential faith*. This is a counterfeit understanding of faith built on personal experience, not the eternal, unchanging truth of Scripture. An example of this type of faith is that because we are sick and showing no signs of improvement, experiential faith begins to assume that God's overall will is sickness for our lives. Or another example is that we believe that God does not want to restore a hurting marriage because we see many examples of people in our lives who ended up getting divorced, even though they prayed for reconciliation.

Experiential faith emerges if we are going through something—a sickness, family problem, addiction, trial, or bondage—and rather than stand on what God's eternal Word says and agree with the solutions presented in Scripture, we start to use our circumstances to define who God is for us. If we don't experience immediate healing, then we start to believe that He is *not* the healer. If restoration in a relationship does not take place overnight, we begin to think that He might *not* be a restorer. This perspective shapes how we end up praying about our problems. Bad reports. Hopeless situations. Impossibilities.

Experiential faith often appears to be the most popular and damaging perspective for us to adopt when it comes to faith. We cannot treat God's character like it changes every time we go through a difficult season or situation. He does not respond one day, only to be silent the next. He does not reveal His nature as Healer, Deliverer, or Restorer on Sunday, only to completely change His character on Monday. Experiential faith is *not* faith at all; it is a counterfeit and denies the constancy of God's eternal nature. It is in direct opposition to what Scripture tells us about the Lord Jesus Christ, who *"is the same yesterday and today and forever"* (Hebrews 13:8 NIV).

Does God use our suffering and sickness for His ultimate glory? Absolutely and thoroughly, as He is the God who refuses to let anything be wasted. The key, however, is being able to appropriately identify *where* our circumstances come from and refusing to let them adjust the way we see God.

Second—and this is what I am pursuing at all costs and the lifestyle Jesus is inviting all of us into—is the lifestyle of *breakthrough faith.* And I have some incredible news for you: this is your inheritance as a believer in the Lord Jesus Christ! Gone is the ridiculous idea that "You don't have enough faith to…" and you name the Scripture-based breakthrough you are believing for. The revelation of breakthrough faith completely destroys the concept of "levels of faith," for every person who has given his or her life to the Lord Jesus Christ has received breakthrough faith. The time has come to learn how to activate it and walk in it as your everyday experience.

## The Ceiling

I am all about building a foundation for true breakthrough faith in our lives. The entire essence of this teaching is based on an account in Mark 2 that I have come to affectionately call "Faith that breaks through the ceiling." The ceiling is whatever stands between you and the promises that God's Word legally authorizes you to possess. Examples of these ceilings include the disappointment of perceived unanswered prayers, circumstances that did not work out, or those downright overwhelming seasons when the phrase "hell on earth" takes on new, personal meaning for us.

Faith does not accept any ceiling or any boundary that prevents us from experiencing God's promises coming to pass in our lives. This is the attitude we will be developing in the pages ahead—one that holds on tight to what God has said in His Word, and refuses to let go until what He said becomes what we experience.

We have become inundated with teaching on faith. Many of us are overwhelmed with Kingdom principles—the how-tos of faith. But when it comes down to the foundational level, many believers are not truly grounded in what they believe about who God is, what the Scriptures say, and the supernatural lifestyle Jesus modeled for us to live. As a result, we become susceptible to embracing the experiential faith that changes every time we face opposition.

We may persevere for a season, but ultimately, when things get to be too overwhelming, we throw in the towel, adjust our theology, and conclude that God might not be interested in getting us through our situation or circumstance. That whole business of transforming impossible situations and bringing Heaven to earth sounds more like pie-in-the-sky ideology than the normal Christian life. This should not be the case at all. I am going to help you activate a faith that can break through any situation, season, or circumstance.

## RESTORING BREAKTHROUGH FAITH

We have been given this tool of faith to release Heaven's solution into every situation that does not line up with God's perfect will for our lives. Heaven contains every solution that will transform the circumstances and challenges we face on earth. The lack we experience is not on God's end. He has everything that we need to enjoy victory in this lifetime. The lack exists on earth because there is a disagreement between two worlds and two different realities. God's will and agenda for created order was completely good and *never* involved a separation between Heaven and earth. Sin created this gulf. But the blood of Jesus made it possible for these two worlds to be reconnected once again. Jesus would have never given us the Lord's Prayer as a model if He was not interested in bringing two worlds together—*on earth as it is in Heaven* (Matthew 6:10).

When something on earth is in disagreement with the culture and climate of Heaven, it should not be okay with us. In fact, it is completely unacceptable. Paul identifies us as ambassadors of the Lord Jesus Christ (2 Corinthians 5:20), representing the culture of Heaven while on earth. Before we are citizens of a country, governmental system, or even the planet Earth, our citizenship was first in Heaven (Philippians 3:20). This citizenship has everything to do with the ultimate purpose of faith, for Christianity is all about bringing Heaven to earth.

The early disciples and followers of Christ recognized this. Every time faith in Christ was demonstrated and released miracles, signs, wonders, and healings, Heaven's culture was being established on earth. Everything that was normal in God's world was coming into this one. This is our primary mission while living on this planet, according to the Lord's Prayer.

I place no restrictions on how much of Heaven is available for here and now. We leave that up to God. In the meantime, we are called to embrace this commission with great joy, knowing that through faith we get to participate in bringing divine alignment between God's solutions and our impossibilities.

Prolific author and prophet Kris Vallotton makes the following comment about the early followers of Christ and their overall mission:

> Apostles are not only sent; they are sent for a very specific purpose. The word "apostle" comes from the secular Roman world. The Romans were very aggressive about expanding their empire. They wisely employed the strategy of Alexander the Great, who established the Greek Empire by conquering kingdoms and then culturizing them in Greek ways.[2]

They were not just disciples—ones who learned from the Master. They were apostles—sent ones, called to culturize planet Earth with the ways and culture of Heaven. This is our mission too! Faith is not only about getting us into Heaven one day, but following the apostles' lead and making our world look as much like Heaven as possible. As ambassadors and emissaries of Christ, Heaven is our place of citizenship, not just an eternal resting place. Heaven can have influence and impact *now*, on earth, in our sphere of influence, through our faith!

## WE ARE EQUIPPED FOR THE TASK

Whatever you think about faith, I ask that you keep an open mind and let the Holy Spirit come and lead you into all truth. My heart burns to see the body of Christ unlock the power of breakthrough faith and bring the supernatural power of Heaven to earth—in our lives and in our world. I want each believer to walk in sustained, consistent victory over the unbiblical circumstances that come against us. These things are not God's sovereign plan or purpose for our lives.

If you are currently dealing with circumstances that are not in line with God's Word—either in your life or someone else's—I want to equip you with practical tools to break through every obstacle, press through every circumstance, and experience victory in every season of your life, in Jesus's name!

## POINT OF BREAKTHROUGH

*We already received breakthrough faith at the moment of our salvation; the key is in understanding what we already possess and activating it to live a lifestyle of sustained victory!*

Faith is not only about getting us into Heaven one day, but following the apostles' lead and making our world look as much like Heaven as possible.

## IDENTIFY THE GREAT DECEPTION

*And when they could not come near Him because of the crowd, they uncovered the roof where He was. So when they had broken through, they let down the bed on which the paralytic was lying* (Mark 2:4 NKJV).

What is the *great deception* I am referring to here? It is simply this: everything that happens in life is God's will. Is says that, "Whatever I experience in life, whether good or bad, is God's divine orchestration and comes directly from His hand." If God wanted us to "take life" lying down, embracing everything that happened to us as His sovereign plan, then He would not have invited us to walk in a supernatural lifestyle of breakthrough faith.

The four men in Mark 2 brought their paralyzed friend to the house where Jesus was teaching. It was so full of people that they could not get inside. They could have seen this opposition as God's sovereign will not to heal their friend. But they had already heard so much about Jesus's miracles and power. They heard about what He did for *everyone* who came to Him, and the testimony they heard about Jesus actually revealed who Jesus was. He was compassionate. He was the Healer. His identity was unchanging, and these men knew that if they got their paralyzed friend into the Presence of the Healer, his situation would be transformed.

They had such strong faith in this Jesus, who miraculously transformed circumstances, that they literally broke through a ceiling and lowered their friend down, right in front of Jesus. Oh, how Jesus loves breakthrough faith!

The "God is in control" approach of everything we go through is a great deception that completely discounts the reality of our enemy, demolishes any opportunity to exercise faith, and dangerously skews the very nature, character, and activity of God. God is truly sovereign, but when it comes to Him manipulating and controlling certain things that take place on planet Earth, we must be aware that there are enemy forces at work too.

When we start attributing things to God that are not His doing, but are instead the result of sin, or, even worse, the direct assault of our enemy, satan, we begin to introduce uncertainty into our relationship with Him because we see His character incorrectly. It's skewed. We try to soothe ourselves by packaging it in silly theological language like, "God has a purpose" or "God has a plan" or "God is good," but deep down, we end up with a pile of unanswered questions that were never designed to go unanswered.

This is not to say that there is no mystery to God and that absolutely everything that happens in life will make total sense. It won't. However, there are some very clear and defined realities we need to settle in our hearts concerning God—who He is, what He's like, and what He does and does not do, if we are to relate to Him properly. We need to identify the true source of pain, torment, and affliction in our lives.

## NOTES

1. If you are not yet a believer in the Lord Jesus Christ, I would encourage you to immediately flip to the Afterword in the back of the book to read more about how to make this glorious, life-changing decision.

2. Kris Vallotton, *Heavy Rain* (Ventura, CA: Regal, 2010), 65.

# RECOGNIZE THE BATTLE

by

*Larry Sparks*

*...lest Satan should take advantage of us; for we are not ignorant of his devices* (2 Corinthians 2:11 NKJV).

We have an enemy. He is not some theological concept. He is more than just bad thoughts and temptations. The devil, satan, is our adversary and antagonist. I don't say this with intention to frighten but rather with a purpose to educate. In view of the enemy's reality and agenda, it is absolutely ridiculous for us to identify *everything* that happens to us as God's sovereign will and perfect plan.

Let me illustrate. Even though the Bible told me there was a real devil and real demons, experientially this did not become an up-close-and-personal reality for me until January 2012. I was at a revival service in Orlando, Florida. Toward the end of the meeting, as the worship team was passionately exalting Jesus and the crowds were experiencing wave after wave of God's glorious Presence, I started walking around the sanctuary praying. As I briefly looked down, I saw a small group of people gathered around a girl. She looked like she was in her twenties. Her eyes were black, her face was contorted, and she was biting herself. Blood was tricking down her arm.

I was amazed at the honor the small group was showing her. They didn't push her up to the platform for some type of public spectacle or highly charged exorcist scenario. In fact, I recall a woman cradling the demonized girl in her arms while the others were quietly praying over her. Out of respect for what God was doing, I moved on quickly as to not dishonor the young woman who was being set free from demonic torment. And praise God, by the time I ran into her and the group later on, she was in her right mind, appearing completely free.

God's perfect will was not for that young woman to be in torment and bondage to some demonic, oppressive spirit. His will happened on the *other side* of that small group of people praying for her, honoring her, loving her, and declaring the Word of God and the power of Jesus's name over her. This was done in faith so that the Spirit of God could set her free. And He did!

## BREAKING OUR AGREEMENT WITH DARKNESS AND WISING UP

Faith is the supernatural force that breaks agreement with the enemy and releases the solutions of Heaven into our circumstances. Again, we see the true nature of faith at work as the power and resources of God's world flow into ours, overriding what the enemy intends for our destruction. When we bow to the enemy's deceptions, we are agreeing with darkness and thereby giving him an open door into our lives.

One of the main ways we agree with darkness is by attributing the work of the enemy to the sovereign will of God. As long as we believe God is causing the destructive, negative, afflicting circumstances in our lives—realities that the Bible clearly attributes to the work of darkness—the longer we will remain in bondage to deception. Instead of combating circumstances in faith, we will simply yield to them, believing they are God's doing.

My book *Breakthrough Faith* was birthed out of a vision to see Christians refuse to get trampled on by the enemy and fight back from a position of victory. When we allow the devil to wreak havoc in our lives, it is not because we are dealing with a worthy opponent; it is because we are actually giving the devil the only power he has available—our agreement.

> Faith is the supernatural force that breaks agreement with the enemy and releases the solutions of Heaven into our circumstances.

Before we explore the foundations of faith, discover what it means to persevere in faith, and position ourselves to receive breakthrough by faith, we need to understand the contrary forces that have been working against the people of God since day one. Do you know what the enemy's great deception is? It is nothing less than ignorance of his involvement in the world. Dr. Jack Graham notes, "That's a central goal of satan's, to make Christians doubt his existence, his power, his prowess in causing destruction in our lives."[1] If the devil's not involved, then everything bad must come from the hand of God.

## ACKNOWLEDGING OUR ENEMY

God does not want us to be ignorant of the devil's sly devices. The serpent of old would love to convince the world that he is some nonexistent, fictitious, fairy-tale figure, that he is the making of Hollywood. Countless Christians actually deny the realities of hell, demons, and a literal devil altogether. The fruit of this deception is absolutely startling because if we do not believe in the contrary forces of darkness, all of the evil and opposition in life ultimately come from the hand of God. We must acknowledge the reality of the devil and his dominion of darkness if we want to experience breakthrough.

This does not make it legal for us to become overly preoccupied with darkness. My pastor always says that there are ditches on both sides of the road—and both of them are bad and should be steered clear of. Unholy preoccupation with darkness is the other ditch the enemy would love us to fall into, where we spend all of our time running after demons, duking it out with the devil, rebuking, renouncing, and delivering—spending so much time on the defense that nothing offensive takes place. Darkness gains ground when it keeps the church living on the defense, but it trembles when a people rise up, armed with faith, recognizing the apostolic potential of their faith.

## MOVING FROM DEFENSE TO OFFENSE

The devil does not tremble at those who are fighting him all of the time. If we are spending most of our Christian lives fighting with the devil, this means we believe some major lies about the devil. The truth is—the devil is defeated and we are victorious! To fight the devil is to fight one who has already been defeated, disarmed, stripped of his power and completely overthrown. A.W. Tozer describes it this way: "I'm not afraid of the devil. The devil can handle me—he's got judo I never heard of. But he can't handle the One to whom I'm joined; he can't handle the One to whom I'm united; he can't handle the One whose nature dwells in my nature."[2] The devil is not frightened of ignorant believers; however, he is absolutely terrified of those who recognize and represent the Victorious One who lives inside them.

> When God Himself becomes the glorious quest of the church, darkness will become subdued in an unprecedented manner.

The whole of hell trembles at the believer who recognizes his or her inheritance, and lives in an offensive posture toward darkness. Again, this does not involve making darkness a focal point. Rather, the knowledge of the Holy One is what feeds and fuels the victorious Christian. The person who makes God his or her main focus, pursuit, and conquest is the very one who will carry Heaven's solutions into every arena of life. When God Himself becomes the glorious quest of the church, darkness will become subdued in an unprecedented manner.

It's time to transition from the defensive to the offensive. Author Francis Frangipane says, "The Spirit of God does not want us to merely tolerate oppression; He desires us to conquer it."[3] This is what putting breakthrough faith into action looks like. Faith is not just about holding down the fort and fighting off the enemy; it is about gaining new ground for God's Kingdom. By studying the Word of God together, I want to help you experience this in your life!

## POINT OF BREAKTHROUGH

*Not everything that happens in our lives is the sovereign will and plan of God. We must recognize the influence of the devil—who is our enemy and adversary—in order to exercise breakthrough faith in every situation we face.*

## NOTES

1. Jack Graham, *Unseen* (Grand Rapids, MI: Bethany House, 2013), 37.

2. A.W. Tozer, *God's Greatest Gift to Man*.

3. Francis Frangipane, *This Day We Fight* (Grand Rapids, MI: Chosen, 2005), 21.

## RECOMMENDED READING

*Unseen* by Dr. Jack Graham

*Happy Intercessor* by Beni Johnson

*Spirit Wars* by Kris Vallotton

*This Day We Fight* by Francis Frangipane

# IDENTIFY YOUR ENEMY

by

*Larry Sparks*

*The first step on the way to victory is to recognize the enemy.* —Corrie Ten Boom[1]

We are in a battle *against* a real enemy. He is real and he is the antagonist of every believer. He is not some figment of Christianity's collective imagination or some guy running around in a red suit with a pitchfork and a tail. We must recognize the enemy's reality if we are to experience the victory God has ordained for us. Otherwise, we will continue to fall right into the devil's trap and attribute all of his works of darkness to providence and the sovereign hand of God.

In this chapter I teach you how to become aware of our enemy without becoming grossly preoccupied with him. Pretending the devil away keeps us believing that God is responsible for all of the problems and circumstances we face, while focusing on the devil too much distracts us from a Christianity of conquest and prevents forward momentum. It makes perfect sense then that the enemy would like nothing more than for us to either make a big deal out of him, believing he is stronger than

God, or believe that he does not exist. Both of these thoughts are lies, and that is all the serpent can ever do—lie. C.S. Lewis put it best in his classic book *The Screwtape Letters*:

> There are two equal and opposite errors into which our race can fall about the devils. One is to disbelieve in their existence. The other is to believe, and to feel an excessive and unhealthy interest in them. They themselves are equally pleased by both errors and hail a materialist or a magician with the same delight.[2]

By entertaining either one of these deceptions, the devil gets what he wants: Christians filled with power and believe they are powerless against the circumstances they encounter. Either God is responsible for all of the bad stuff or the devil is this overwhelming, super-strong adversary we will spend our entire lives battling against, and always losing. In the previous chapter we discussed the danger of neglecting the truth of our enemy, but we can also overemphasize him too.

## DON'T GIVE THE DEVIL TOO MUCH CREDIT

I don't want us to invest too much emphasis on the devil here. He's simply not worth our time. However, we need to be informed about who we are dealing with if we are going to approach faith the right way. These truths are absolutely foundational because, unfortunately, there are so many believers out there who hold to an orthodox view of Scripture and mentally assent to the reality of the devil and demons. However, they fail to recognize their involvement in humanity and they don't really grasp the enemy's sinister agenda against every person on the planet. We need to study the following topic with balance and wisdom in order to walk in the victory that breakthrough faith releases.

As a middle schooler, I was intrigued by horror movies, particularly the supernatural ones—*The Omen, The Exorcist, Rosemary's Baby*, etc. In the last decade, the only thing that has changed are the titles and increasingly graphic nature of gore, sexuality, and darkness present on the movie screen. A generation is still being enticed by the works of darkness. Why is this?

This is because there appears to be power available in the darkness. Once again, the devil is taking his place as the author of lies, because the only power he has is what we give him. When the prince of darkness is the front and center of our focus, he becomes powerful. He becomes a formidable foe, not because he actually is, but because of our emphasis and focus upon him. The devil only gets scary when we believe that he is.

> Pretending the devil away keeps us believing that God is responsible for all of the problems and circumstances we face, while focusing on the devil too much distracts us from a Christianity of conquest and prevents forward momentum.

The reality is our enemy is a defeated foe, crushed under the feet of King Jesus. This is why he uses media, television, and Hollywood to try and convince the world, and yes, even deceive believers into thinking he is more frightening and powerful than he really is. This is simply not the case. When it comes to exercising breakthrough faith, if we are under the assumption that the devil is a force to be reckoned with, we are going to live in defense mode rather than on the offense.

Preachers, teachers, evangelists, and anyone involved in ministry can easily fall prey to this overemphasis of the devil as well. We just make it sound more spiritual than watching horror movies—but I believe it is as equally dangerous! Perry Stone gives a fantastic illustration in his book *Exposing Satan's Playbook*, where his mother actually tried to run a spiritual intervention for him. She went to a key leader in the ministry and expressed her concerns about Perry, noting that since he became obsessed with studying the demonic, all sorts of unusual phenomena had plagued him. Horrible things started happening, including actual "visible manifestations of spirits cloaked in dark garments and hoods and hiding their faces."[3]

The devil does whatever he can to convince us of his non-existence or insidiously draw us into his world of darkness through intrigue. Perry Stone shares the exceptional advice that this ministry leader gave him: "As long as you concentrate on demons, they will show up. If you preach and concentrate on Jesus, then He will show up."[4] That statement makes me want to shout!

So Perry made a shift in his emphasis, from darkness to light, from focusing on the devil to keeping Jesus at the center of all things. He concluded that as a result of the shift in focus, "the presence of Christ began to manifest and deliver individuals from the oppression of the enemy."[5] Interestingly enough, overemphasis on the devil and his demons

> Our enemy is a defeated foe, crushed under the feet of King Jesus.

does not bring deliverance to those in torment and captivity. When we give the enemy more attention than he is due, we end up exaggerating his power. This actually keeps people in bondage and torment, rather than introducing these individuals to the Author of freedom, hope, and healing—Jesus Christ.

After learning this valuable lesson, Perry Stone gives us a powerful key to activating our breakthrough faith and releasing the supernatural power of God: we are to shift focus from the defeated one who deceives with trickery and illusions and exalt the Greater One living inside us, who has all authority, all power, and all dominion. Darkness does not stand a chance in the Presence of King Jesus!

## Basic Facts about Our Enemy

With all of this in mind, there are some basic facts we need to keep in mind concerning the adversary if we want to begin living a lifestyle of breakthrough faith. Peter reminds us, *"Be sober, be vigilant; because your adversary the devil walks about like a roaring lion, seeking whom he may devour"* (1 Peter 5:8 NKJV).

### The Enemy Is Our Adversary

The devil is not God's adversary, as God already defeated him at the cross of Calvary. Rather, he is *our* adversary. The Amplified Bible's wording of 1 Peter 5:8 emphasizes Peter acknowledging this, writing *"for that enemy of yours, the devil...."* The very name satan, in Hebrew, means "adversary."[6] His tactics are not aimed at God; they are rather directed toward us. After all, God is not going to believe the devil's lies; the only ones capable of believing his deceptions and thereby granting him an inroad into their lives are human beings, like you and me. This is not intended to scare you; it is only meant to simply raise awareness that your adversary is not God but the devil.

## The Enemy Is a Devourer

God is not the One who devours and destroys—this job description belongs to the devil, as Peter makes so abundantly clear in 1 Peter 5:8. It is vital that we classify anything that threatens to destroy life or assault the promises of God as devilish in origin.

## The Enemy Devours Those Who Allow Him

There is a secret in this Scripture verse that arms us for victory. Unfortunately, it gets lost amidst us focusing on the devil, his evil schemes, and his being like a lion (he is *not* a lion; he only masquerades as one). Peter tells us that the devil is *"seeking whom he may devour,"* with the key word being *may*. In this book, you will be armed to stare down the devil's tactics in the face and with burning words of faith declare, "No, you *may* not!" We must stop giving him permission to devour our lives.

## The Enemy Is Our Foe and Antagonist

Ephesians 6 reminds us that we are in a battle. Paul writes:

> *Put on the whole armor of God, that you may be able to stand against the wiles of the devil. For we do not wrestle against flesh and blood, but against principalities, against powers, against the rulers of the darkness of this age, against spiritual hosts of wickedness in the heavenly places* (Ephesians 6:11-12 NKJV).

The devil is defeated, but nevertheless he is looking for an inroad of agreement because he is well aware of the destruction he can bring to lives that say yes to his deceptions. Paul reminds us to be on guard—not against our Father God who is out to get us, but rather against the strategies of the devil, the *evil one* (see Matthew 6:13; John 17:15; 2 Thessalonians 3:3). You may chuckle at that, but we seriously need a paradigm adjustment if we are going to walk in supernatural, breakthrough faith. The devil is our enemy, not our Father. God is not fighting against us; He is fighting *for* us, equipping us with every resource necessary to stand victorious in the day of battle! (See Romans 8:31.) The fight is fixed and the battle is already won.

## The Enemy Is No Respecter of Innocence

The enemy respects no one. This is obvious in a world stained by child abuse, sex trafficking, and the unspeakable atrocities committed against the innocent. It is easy to let these realities cause us to desire a speedy return of Christ. The reality is, however, that while we are still occupying planet Earth, we must recognize that these abominations are the by-products of a devil who is deceiving people left and right, obtaining an inroad into their lives, gaining a foothold, developing a stronghold, and ultimately achieving a stranglehold. Again, we must acknowledge the horrors in this world as the devil's architecture, otherwise we begin to distort and pervert the good character of God.

## The Enemy Is Our Accuser

John writes in the Book of Revelation that the devil, who is *"the accuser of our brothers and sisters, who accuses them before our God day and night, has been hurled down"* (Revelation 12:10 NIV). This Scripture reveals two realities when it comes to the devil being our accuser. The

> God is not fighting against us; He is fighting for us, equipping us with every resource necessary to stand victorious in the day of battle.

first is that the devil no longer accuses us before God; rather, he accuses us directly.

Do you know why he is unable to accuse us before God, bringing up our sin, our works, our issues, and our unworthiness before the throne of Heaven? It is because he knows that God would have one eternal response to each one of the enemy's accusations—the blood of Jesus was enough.

In the book of Job we see the devil presenting Job before God (see Job 1:6-12), but I do not believe that such a scenario is possible under the New Covenant. While the enemy cannot accuse us before God, he can accuse us directly and try to deceive us out of believing that the blood of Jesus is enough to make us acceptable in God's sight. I believe this is the chief revelation that he will try to challenge in our life, for it is Jesus's blood and our testimony that ultimately spell defeat for him.

## POINT OF BREAKTHROUGH

*We recognize the enemy's tactics,*
*not to become overly preoccupied with darkness,*
*but to predict his moves and thwart his advances in our lives.*

## NOTES

1.  Martin H. Manser, *The Westminster Collection of Christian Quotations* (Louisville, KY: Westminster John Knox Press, 2001), 390.

2.  C.S. Lewis, *The Screwtape Letters*.

3.  Perry Stone, *Exposing Satan's Playbook* (Lake Mark: Charisma House, 2012), 153.

4.  Ibid.

5.  Ibid.

6.  Wayne Grudem, *Systematic Theology* (Grand Rapids, MI: Zondervan), 414.

## RECOMMENDED READING

*The Screwtape Letters* by C.S. Lewis

*Exposing Satan's Playbook* by Perry Stone

*Eight Ways to Keep the Devil Under Your Feet* by Joyce Meyer

4

# HIS GOODNESS—
# HIS GLORY

by

*Bill Johnson*

*You become like what you worship. When you gaze
in awe, admiration, and wonder at something or
someone, you begin to take on something of the character
of the object of your worship.* —N.T. Wright

The Law of Moses was but for a season. It was never meant to carry the full manifestation of God's nature to be discovered and enjoyed by His people. While it was necessary and beautiful, it fell far short in representing the Father's heart. That was not its purpose. The Law taught Israel what they needed to know about the Messiah before He came upon the scene. And even then, most missed His coming. And yet riddled all throughout God's dealings with His people in the Old Testament was the revelation of grace. Some of the most beautiful glimpses of God's heart are hidden in the scenes of the Old Testament. There are great differences between law and grace. But for now, this will suffice—law requires, while grace enables.

God illustrated His heart for His people over and over again. He declared, *"Say to them, 'As I live!' declares the Lord God, 'I take no pleasure in the death of the wicked, but rather that the wicked turn from his way and live. Turn back, turn back from your evil ways! Why then will you die, O house of Israel?'"* (Ezekiel 33:11 NASB). God is not an angry tyrant wishing evil people to be punished and die. If that were true, it would have happened long before now, released through a simple decree. Instead, we see Him interceding so that the wicked would turn and live. His passion for all of us is to experience life to the fullest! But it is never forced upon us; otherwise, He ends up with robots, not people made in His image.

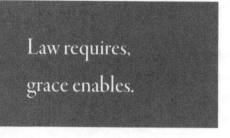

Law requires, grace enables.

One of the most treasured portions of Old Testament Scripture is the blessing God told Moses to pass on to Aaron to declare over His people (Numbers 6:22-27). Obviously, God can bless whomever He wants, whenever He wants. But He longed for His people to know His heart for them. He also wanted it to be spoken, as something happens when we join our words with His heart.

Aaron was the high priest, and as such he was positioned to release the blessing of God over the people. God wanted blessing declared over His people every day of their lives. It was to be declared because what is spoken makes a difference. This was not simply a formality. Everything God tells us to do has great significance. This is a picture of the high priest joining his heart with the heart of God—to release the reality of His Kingdom into the lives of His people through decree. We live with the conviction that nothing happens in the Kingdom of God until something is spoken. This passage reveals His passion for His people to know of His love, His bounty, and His all sufficiency. This is the heart of God for us all:

> And the Lord spoke to Moses, saying, "Speak to Aaron and his sons, saying, 'This is the way you shall bless the children of Israel. Say to them: "The Lord bless you and keep you; the Lord make His face shine upon you, and be gracious to you; the Lord lift up His countenance upon you, and give you peace."' So they shall put My name on the children of Israel, and I will bless them" (Numbers 6:22-27 NKJV).

*What we believe about God will have an effect on our lives in a measurable way because He rewards those who have set their hearts on discovering Him.*

## THE GOD JOURNEY

God invites us to discover Him, the One who rewards all who join in the journey into the great expanse called the goodness of God. This is the journey of faith, for faith believes *"that He is, and that He is a rewarder of those who diligently seek Him"* (Hebrews 11:6 NKJV). Faith has two parts; the first is a conviction of His existence. But even the devil has that much going for him. It's the second part that launches us into the adventure and distinguishes us from the rest of all that exists—a confidence in His nature. He is the rewarder!

> Real faith is superior to the human intellect in that it is the product of God's mind instead of ours.

In other words, what we believe about Him will have an effect on our lives in a measurable way because He rewards those who have set their hearts on discovering Him. He promises, *"You will seek Me...and I will be found by you!"* (Jeremiah 29:13-14 NKJV). God ensures that we find Him if the heart is genuinely searching with a readiness to obey. Jesus also said He would disclose Himself to those who follow Him (see John 14:21). It's as though He is saying that if we seek Him with all of our hearts, He will make sure to put Himself in the middle of the road we're walking on.

This invitation comes from the Father of life—the eternal God who loves through sacrifice and giving. The greatest gift we could ever give ourselves is to anchor our intellect and will into the strongest foundation possible—the goodness of God.

This voyage is one of faith. Faith is considered to be anti-intellectual by many. It is not. In reality, it enhances the intellect but is vastly superior, for faith is able to recognize the unseen world that the natural mind has little place for. Real faith is superior to the human intellect in that it is the product of God's mind instead of ours. Faith comes from the heart, one that lives under the influence of God's mind.

Faith is the result of surrender, not self-will. It's more correctly stated that our intellect is shaped and influenced by authentic faith, for true faith precedes understanding on eternal matters, like those pertaining to the unseen world. *"By faith we understand that the worlds were framed by the word of God, so that the things which are seen were not made of things which are visible"* (Hebrews 11:3 NKJV). Take note that it is faith that enables us to understand the unseen world, which according to the apostle Paul is eternal, while the things we see are temporal. (See 2 Corinthians 4:18.) So faith then anchors us into the substance of eternity, a solid footing for sure. By faith we understand, for it is faith that enhances the intellect.

My faith can go only where I have understanding of His goodness. His goodness then becomes the real estate that I live on and explore freely. He liberally gives us all He is and all He has. (See John 16:14-15.) Biblical faith explores this realm with the delight and pleasure of a well-loved child. Jesus teaches that the Kingdom of God belongs to those who are like children. Adults tend to manage what they have, taking fewer and fewer risks as they get older. But children tirelessly explore. When our faith explores His goodness, we are most like the children Jesus honored and celebrated. (See Mark 10:14.)

## THE ADVENTURE INTO THE EXTREME

Everything about God is extreme in the best possible sense. He is infinitely good, infinitely holy and powerful, infinitely beautiful, magnificent, and glorious. These are just a few terms to describe Him. But none of the endless lists of traits and characteristics confine Him. Religion, which I define as *form without power*, tends to attempt the impossible task of restricting Him into neat little packages, giving us a false sense of intelligence and ultimately

> My faith can go only where I have understanding of His goodness.

control. But He is bigger and bigger and bigger still. Each virtue gives us a glimpse into that which is beyond measure but is open for observation. You could take one trait and explore it for all of eternity but not come close to exhausting the depths of who He is in that particular virtue.

History is filled with the stories of explorers and their adventures. Whether it's the quest of a Columbus to go where no European had gone before, or the astronauts who travel through space, or the intellectually curious of our day exploring the depths of science, medicine, and technology, we have been given the drive to search for more. God invites us into these quests as a part of our God-given nature to discover and create. His gifts of curiosity and desire are beautiful expressions of His heart as a Father.

George Washington Carver used this drive to discover things that would ultimately help the poor he lived to serve. His passion to unveil the secrets of creation began with his research on the peanut. He was known for his absolute faith in God as the cornerstone of his research and is credited with discovering over three hundred uses for the peanut. He claimed that it was faith that "held all inquiry and action accountable."[1] The impact of his research reached far and wide, but his primary target was to benefit the poor. As a result, this one man is credited with having an amazing impact on the economy of the southern states in the US, all because he believed God rewards those who seek Him.

## HIDE AND SEEK

Solomon, the man known for unequalled wisdom, made this declaration: *"It is the glory of God to conceal a matter, but the glory of kings is to search out a matter"* (Proverbs 25:2 NKJV). I find it fascinating that God is glorified by concealing or hiding things. But it must be understood that He hides things for us, not from us.

My wife, Beni, and I have nine grandchildren. On Easter we hide eggs for them in our front yard. While I've never been able to figure out what a bunny and eggs have to do with the resurrection of Jesus, we still love hiding eggs for the children in our lives. It is just another excuse to have fun with our family. That being said, I would never dig a three-foot hole in the ground, put in the various kinds of eggs we use into the bottom of the hole, and then cover it with cement. Can you imagine me telling our grandchildren, "If you think you're so smart, try to find those eggs." Hardly. We hide the eggs to be found. There's no joy in putting something out of their reach. Our joy is in their discovery.

All the adults cheer for them to find what's been hidden. We yell out when they're close. We'll even tell them to turn this way or that, or look higher or lower. We would never think of going into the house while they hunt for these treasures outside. They have great joy in finding the eggs. But they also look back at us, making sure we are watching. Part of their joy is in our joy over them. Our grandchildren range from five to sixteen years of age. (The three oldest ones, fourteen to sixteen years old, now help the younger ones to be successful.) We put some eggs in very hard places and others out in the open. The older ones know that if the egg is "hidden in the open," it's for one of the younger ones.

When they were two years old, we'd put the brightly colored treasures on the steps, or on the bricks, or on the driveway next to a car tire. The eggs were hidden in the open so they'd be found. But if we put all the eggs in the open, the older ones would have no fun at all. They'd rightfully complain about our lack of effort to make it challenging for them. Their maturity requires that we take more thought in where we hide the eggs. Remember, the goal is joy, fun, and pleasure in the context of family. This simple illustration wonderfully represents our discovery of His goodness and speaks of His delight in our discovery. He truly is glorified in concealing a matter for us to find.

In the same way, the Father draws us into the journey of discovering His nature. His entire realm of dominion called the Kingdom of God is hidden for us to find. It is an eternal Kingdom in which all of eternity will be needed to discover what He has made for us.

The second part of the Proverbs 25:2 passage is equally important to the first part: *"the glory of kings is to search out a matter."* We have been created in the image of God, the King of all kings. We are royalty. Our royalty is never more at the forefront of our lives than when we live with the conviction that God has given us legal access to all things, including the hidden things—mysteries. And so we ask, seek, and knock, knowing there will be a breakthrough. (See Matthew 7:7-8.) Some of the things in this Kingdom are discovered almost without looking. They seem to find us. And yet other breakthroughs seem to take the better part of a lifetime. This joyful adventure begins now, but it will continue throughout all eternity.

## THE LAND OF GOODNESS

We are all explorers, searching for the new, enjoying the old, becoming personally enlarged with each discovery. What we behold affects us. If we look at it long enough, it changes us. There are parts of God's goodness that are easily noticeable to the casual observer. Much like Moses, we've been given a challenge. He saw a burning bush that wasn't being consumed by its flames. The story records an important detail that should help us all in our journey. It was only when Moses turned aside that the Lord spoke to him from the bush. (See Exodus 3:4.) Sometimes giving undivided attention to the obvious releases a greater encounter with Him, manifesting a greater revelation of what He is like. The bottom line is that we can't find anything significant on our own. It must be revealed to us. In other words, all discoveries are not the result of our discipline and determination alone. As the ultimate steward, He gives these gifts to those who have embraced His invitation to ask, seek, and knock.

The prophet Jeremiah caught a glimpse of this reality when God gave him a promise of restoration. *"Call to Me and I will answer you, and I will tell you great and mighty things, which you do not know"* (Jeremiah 33:3 NASB).

> The Father draws us into the journey of discovering His nature. His entire realm of dominion called the Kingdom of God is hidden for us to find.

The God who is good gave us the invitation to call upon Him. He then promised to answer in a way that was beyond what we asked for. The word *great* in this verse means "considerably above average." And if that weren't enough, He follows the word *great* with the word *mighty*. *Mighty* means "inaccessible."

Consider this: God has given us access to the inaccessible. What an incomprehensible promise! It is out of the reach of our skills, character, or qualifications. We lack all that is necessary to be able to apprehend what exists in the realm called the goodness of God. But He gave us something that makes this impossibility possible. He gave us the key to the inaccessible. He Himself is that key. Through His name we have access to that which is beyond our reach on our best day. The invitation came from His goodness. He invites us to call upon Him, giving Him the open door to answer in a way that is above our expectations and imagination. There is no goodness apart from Him, so our journey is a discovery of the person of God—the One whose inaccessible goodness is now accessible by an invitation with His promise *to be found by us*.

## EXPLORERS UNITE!

Like the adventurers of old, we have before us the most unexplored territory in existence. It is more rugged than Mount Everest, more intimidating than the deepest ocean, and vaster than space itself—it's called God's goodness. We've been invited by God Himself to come taste and see. He has also given us a tour guide to lead and assist us in this journey—the Holy Spirit. He has been given to lead us into all truth, which is always to manifest in freedom.

Once again, we look to Moses, the one to whom the Law was given. In one of his encounters with God, we see an example of grace that creates a high watermark, even by New Testament standards. The apostle Paul mentions it in 2 Corinthians 3:7-18, announcing that this glorious moment was less than what the New Covenant provided for each believer. The New Covenant is better than the Old, and therefore must provide superior blessings and breakthroughs.

In Exodus 33, we find Moses asking God not to send an angel to go with Israel into the Promised Land. He wanted God Himself to go. In fact, Moses stated that if God wasn't going to go, then he didn't want to go, either. This really is quite remarkable. The angel assigned to lead them would have provided everything that God promised. It would have been a fulfillment of all their dreams and aspirations as a nation. And

I remind you that angels carry a certain majesty and glory that is often mistaken for God Himself. Yet Moses had a relationship with God, forged through his trials. God said of Moses, *"The Lord used to speak to Moses face to face, just as a man speaks to his friend"* (Exodus 33:11 NASB). As a friend of God, Moses wanted only to be led by his Friend. The blessings were not the objective. The relationship was.

> *The Lord said to Moses, "I will also do this thing of which you have spoken; for you have found favor in My sight and I have known you by name." Then Moses said, "I pray You, show me Your glory!" And He said, "I Myself will make all My goodness pass before you, and will proclaim the name of the Lord before you; and I will be gracious to whom I will be gracious, and will show compassion on whom I will show compassion." But He said, "You cannot see My face, for no man can see Me and live!" Then the Lord said, "Behold, there is a place by Me, and you shall stand there on the rock; and it will come about, while My glory is passing by, that I will put you in the cleft of the rock and cover you with My hand until I have passed by. Then I will take My hand away and you shall see My back, but My face shall not be seen"* (Exodus 33:17-23 NASB).

When Moses asked to see the glory of God, he did not choose some random aspect of God's person or nature. He chose the original target for every person alive. We were created and designed to live in the glory of God, which is the manifested presence of Jesus. The Scripture says, *"For all have sinned and fall short of the glory of God"* (Romans 3:23 NKJV). Sin caused us to fall short of God's intended target. *To sin* means "to miss the mark." Consider an archer shooting an arrow at a target and then watching that arrow not even reach the target, let alone hit the bull's-eye. That is what our sin has done. We not only missed the

> We were created and designed to live in the glory of God, which is the manifested presence of Jesus.

mark; we didn't even reach the target. But take note of the target—it is the glory of God. We were created to live in that realm. Moses knew it instinctively and longed to see it more clearly.

Consider all the encounters that Moses had with God. The glory of God was present in the burning bush, during the many times on the mountain where God descended upon Moses and spoke, and through the visitations in the tent of meeting, which was also filled with His glory. These are just a few of the examples listed in Scripture. Yet in this moment there was only one thing in his mind—the glory. All of those encounters had an effect on Moses, and then upon Israel. Once you've tasted of the real reason that you're alive, nothing else will ever satisfy. But this particular encounter with God in His glory is the only time Moses' face shone like God's. I think it's important to notice what was unique about this encounter. It's the only time people feared the appearance of Moses, and they had him put a cloth over his head to protect them from what they were seeing upon him. I have this deep personal sense that the glory of God will be a primary subject and passion of the Church in the coming years.

> It came about when Moses was coming down from Mount Sinai (and the two tablets of the testimony were in Moses' hand as he was coming down from the mountain), that Moses did not know that **the skin of his face shone because of his speaking with Him.** So when Aaron and all the sons of Israel

*saw Moses, behold, **the skin of his face shone, and they
were afraid to come near him.** Then Moses called to them,
and Aaron and all the rulers in the congregation returned to
him; and Moses spoke to them. Afterward all the sons of Israel
came near, and he commanded them to do everything that
the Lord had spoken to him on Mount Sinai. **When Moses
had finished speaking with them, he put a veil over his face***
(Exodus 34:29-33 NASB).

Moses asked to see God's glory. God said "okay" and showed Moses
His *goodness*. Take note! It was His goodness that changed Moses' countenance. This, the one time Moses' own countenance was changed, was
only after a fresh revelation of God's goodness. Is this not what is missing
in the New Testament Church? Is it possible that God intends to change
the countenance of His people by a fresh revelation of His goodness?
I think so. The world has seen a divided Church, an angry Church, a
materialistic Church, and the list goes on. What would happen if they
were to see a Church whose very countenance has been transformed by
seeing Him, His glory—His goodness? This is what the world is crying
for; they want to believe it's true—God
is good. How we behold Him is what
makes this a possibility.

## DWELLING IN THE GLORY!

Another favorite story of mine also has
to do with the glory of God. Ever since
my dad taught us what it meant for us
to be priests unto the Lord, ministering

> Once you've tasted
> of the real reason
> that you're alive,
> nothing else will
> ever satisfy.

49

to Him with our thanksgiving, praise, and worship, I have embraced this as a primary purpose for my life. Every time I read in Scripture that there are people ministering to Him and then there's a response from Heaven, I get excited. The lessons are always profound, as there's something of eternity on those moments. It doesn't matter whether it happened with David, Moses, or someone in the New Testament; those interactions are eternal in nature. And so it is with this next story.

> *It came even to pass, as the trumpeters and singers were as one, to make one sound to be heard in praising and thanking the Lord; and **when they lifted up their voice** with the trumpets and cymbals and instruments of music, **and praised the Lord, saying, For he is good**; for his mercy endureth for ever: that **then the house was filled with a cloud**, even the house of the Lord; so that the priests could not stand to minister by reason of the cloud: for **the glory of the Lord had filled the house of God** (2 Chronicles 5:13-14 KJV).*

Please note that the priests were offering the fruit of the lips (see Hebrews 13:15) as their offering. While this happened in the Old Testament, it is clearly a New Testament practice, as the Law required the sacrifice of animals from the priests, not praise. Second, notice that the priests were in unity. Remember that the 120 believers in Acts chapters 1 and 2 were also in unity before the outpouring of the Holy Spirit took place. God once again put His glory upon a united people. (See Psalm 133.) God loves to manifest Himself upon His people when we're known for our love of each other.

Third, look at what they were praising God for—His goodness! They declared the Lord to be good! Once again we see a connection between the revelation of His goodness and His glory—His manifested presence. This is amazing, as the glory of God is to cover the earth as the waters cover the sea before time comes to an end (see Habakkuk 2:14). I suppose that many think this glory will become manifest through a military move of the return of the Messiah. His disciples thought that, too. (See Luke 19:11-17.) But I'd like to suggest that in the same way that the disciples were wrong about this, so we, too, are wrong, as we often fail to understand the process He loves to work through. He longs for our involvement in all these matters. Not because He needs us. Co-laboring has been His heart from the beginning. And becoming a worshiping community that worships in spirit, in truth, and in unity will offer something to Him that He in turn will want to occupy—the praises of His people concerning His goodness.

I remember a number of years ago we had a prophetic song during one of our Sunday morning services. We call this type of song "the song of the Lord" in that it is a prophetic song, sung as though it were His voice singing over us as His people. It went something like this:

> Did I not fill the tabernacle of Moses with My glory?
> Did I not fill the temple of Solomon with My glory?
> How much more should I fill the place that I build with My own hands?

God was not ashamed to put His glory upon and in the physical buildings that people built in honor of His name. How much more will He put the glory in the house that He Himself builds?

> If the glory of God contains the revelation of the goodness of God, then here is a key. Jesus Christ dwelling in us by the Holy Spirit is what makes the revelation of His goodness known to and through us to the world around us. And that is hope illustrated.

My beloved, I am building you.

In that moment we realized that God was referring to the Matthew 16:18 (NKJV) passage where Jesus said, *"I will build My church."* So here it is, a chance to catch a glimpse of where God puts His glory and why. He was not ashamed to put His glory upon and in the physical buildings that people built in honor of His name. How much more will He put the glory in the house that He Himself builds? And that house is the *Church*—the eternal dwelling place of God. (See Ephesians 2:22.) Obviously, I make no references to institutions or buildings when I say "Church." Those elements are good and useful tools of the actual Church. But they in themselves are not the Church.

The Church is comprised of born-again believers who are as living stones, brought together into a spiritual house, to house a priesthood that will offer spiritual sacrifices, acceptable through Jesus. That is the revelation that Peter carried for us. (See 1 Peter 2:5.) I remind you that many consider Peter to be the foundation of the ministry of the Church. (See Matthew 16:18.) And to take it one step further, the glory that is put within that house is to manifest the goodness of God, or we miss the point altogether.

## THE HOPE OF GLORY

The focus of the prophets, as well as the prophetic experiences contained throughout the Scriptures, oftentimes point to God's purposes for His people, the Church. The stories mentioned here reveal God's heart and plans for us. He has purposed to manifest Himself upon us and through us and, as a result, to transform the nature of the world around us. This must be seen, embraced, and received as part of our *reason for being*.

The target of the Lord for us is still the glory. His glory is to become the dwelling place of God's people, as He in turn dwells in us. The apostle Paul used a phrase that is to grab our hearts: *"Christ in you, the hope of glory"* (Colossians 1:27 NKJV). Jesus Christ in us makes it possible to be restored fully to His purpose for us—living in the glory. If the glory of God contains the revelation of the goodness of God, then here is a key. Jesus Christ dwelling in us by the Holy Spirit is what makes the revelation of His goodness known to and through us to the world around us. And that is hope illustrated.

## TRUSTING IN HIS GOODNESS

From my perspective, Psalm 27 is one of the most unusual and complete psalms in the Bible. It's a personal favorite. And as such, it has been a wonderful feeding place for my soul for many years. The writer illustrates his absolute trust in God (verses 1-3), the supreme value for His presence (verses 4-6), and his own devotion to obedience (verses 7-10). But the grand finale is the unveiling of his personal secret to strength (verses 11-14). He put it this way in verse 13: *"I would have despaired unless I had believed that I would see the goodness of the Lord in the land of the living"* (NASB). It was his hope of seeing the goodness of God in his day that kept him from hopelessness.

Hopelessness is a thief, one that is often welcomed into Christian circles in the name of discernment. This deceptive influence must be marked and recognized as a tool of the enemy. If ever there was a season in all of history when the people of God need to believe we'll see the glory of God, it is now. God's people are to be known for their hope, regardless of circumstances, perhaps more than most any other virtue.

As one of our own, Olivia Shupe, once observed, "The one with the most hope will always have the most influence." And we have good reason for it! God's goodness wreaks havoc on despair, depression, and hopelessness. Seeing His goodness releases the opportunity for faith. Expecting to taste and see His goodness keeps us impervious to the mental and emotional breakdowns that violate who He designed us to be—carriers of hope, and models of His goodness.

## THE MESSAGE MUST BE DECREED

I owe people the message of the Gospel of the Kingdom of God. It must be declared. This wonderful message includes the good news of salvation for lost and broken humanity, which is all of us. But it is much bigger than that. It is the proclamation of God's rule over everything that exists, in the natural realm as well as the spiritual. And all of that is in the *here and now.* Whatever He rules over has life, freedom, beauty, and order. The decree itself is important because some things don't manifest until they are spoken. If we realized how what we say attracts spiritual reinforcements, angelic or demonic, we'd be much more careful to watch what we say. We'd also be more deliberate in proclaiming what is true—God is in charge and longs to manifest His goodness everywhere.

We sometimes make the mistake of thinking that if we believe the right things, then everything will work out fine. While right beliefs are essential, there is more. So many of the breakthroughs in Scripture would not have happened if the people hadn't declared what God told them to declare. Jesus told us, *"Whoever says to this mountain, 'Be taken up and cast into the sea,' and does not doubt in his heart, but believes that what he says is going to happen, it will be granted him"* (Mark 11:23 NASB). The concept taught here by Jesus is modeled in both the Old and New Testaments. Bold declarations are important. (I realize that the principles of confession and decree have been misused. But the idea of avoiding this truth because of others' errors is akin to refusing to use any currency because counterfeits exist. Misuse by others does not justify no use by me.)

It is good news. It must be preached. *"How then will they call on Him in whom they have not believed? How will they believe in Him whom they have not heard? And how will they hear without a preacher?"* (Romans 10:14 NASB). The message of the Kingdom is received with repentance. People must turn from their sin and put their faith in the Son of God. Treating sin lightly doesn't help the people we're serving. Confession of sin is coming into agreement with God about our need for forgiveness and our hopeless condition apart from Jesus. Because repentance means to change the way we think, the sorrow for sin must be deep enough to provoke an inward change in our perspective on reality. We must keep it real.

The message of the Kingdom is what Jesus preached, and to illustrate that it was for His followers, too, Paul preached it. At the end of the book of Acts is the following statement that summarizes the message of this apostle's life: *"And he stayed two full years in his own rented quarters and was welcoming all who came to him,* **preaching the kingdom of God** *and teaching concerning the* **Lord** *Jesus Christ with all openness, unhindered"* (Acts 28:30-31 NASB).

Boldness in preaching this message attracts Heaven. The record of Scripture demonstrates how God responds to the bold declaration of the Gospel. (See Acts 4:28-29.) It's beautiful. But still many don't take this mandate seriously because the message of God ruling over us seems so invasive. In this case, we, the messengers, must repent before we can expect the people to repent. It's wrong thinking that must change.

The concept of ruling is offensive because of the abuses of power-hungry people. But abusive people do not illustrate or define God. They rule for their own benefit as they rule out of fear instead of love. If we understood the goodness of God, this subject of a King who rules over us would bring great joy to our hearts. He is the model for all government, displaying His two basic purposes—ruling and serving.

Those principles apply to all rulership, whether it's over a nation, business, home, or whatever. First we *rule to protect*, and second we *serve to empower*. Peter gives us the following charge: *"Submit yourselves for the Lord's sake to every human institution, whether to a king as the one in authority, or to governors as sent by him for the* **punishment of evildoers** *and the* **praise of those who do right"** (1 Peter 2:13-14 NASB). The *punishment of evildoers* is the protection part of this equation. *Punishment* brings justice and restitution to the victim, creating boundaries for ongoing protection. The *praise of those who do right* is the empowering part of governing. Leading this way gives attention to what you want to increase in the land if you're a political leader, and in your home if you're a parent.

The honor that comes from leaders goes a long way in establishing the grounds for promotion and increase as a healthy part of our culture. Deep personal fulfillment comes to everyone when there is this kind of righteous leadership. These two elements are to be the main responsibilities of all government, with the Kingdom of God being the ultimate example. For this reason, our message of *"the Kingdom of God is at hand"* is to bring great delight because we know the liberty it brings (Mark 1:15 NKJV). We also know that Jesus is the desire of all nations. (See Haggai 2:7.) That being said, the bold declaration of this message brings the only possible solution to the inward cry of everyone we know.

## NOTE

1. "Legacy of Dr. George Washington Carver: Scientist Extraordinaire, Man of Faith, Educator and Humanitarian," https://www.tuskegee.edu/support-tu/george-washington-carver; accessed January 18, 2023.

# 5

# YOUR VOICE IS POWERFUL

by

*Jodie Hughes*

*...Open **your** mouth with a mighty decree; I
will fulfill it now, you'll see! The words that **you**
speak, so shall it be!* (Psalm 81:10 TPT)

*Receive this truth: Whatever **you** forbid on earth
will be considered to be forbidden in heaven, and
whatever **you** release on earth will be considered to
be released in heaven* (Matthew 18:18 TPT).

Your voice. Your decrees. Your words. Your faith. Your prayers are affecting change!

"Charge your weapons, bride of Christ, and receive this truth." I have heard this phrase over and over in my spirit lately, as the King announces this truth upgrade. Whatever *you* forbid and *you* release will be considered forbidden or released! *You* are empowered and powerful. *You* are called to partner with God's Word and impact what is released from Heaven on the earth. Your voice is essential and part of the process.

The enemy has tried to steal your voice for far too long; and in this season, the shackles are coming off! Get ready, mighty one! Intimidation is breaking across the body of Christ as fresh authority comes on the interceding prophetic voice of the Church.

> *You will also decree a thing, and it will be established for you...* (Job 22:28 NASB).

Your voice is being raised up in new power to declare and establish. God is restoring your story and writing new redemptive solutions into your destiny as you move in faith and decree His promises.

All that the enemy has stolen, messed with, or broken, God is redeeming. New stories of "things working together for good" are being written even now, in the places that felt forgotten or unredeemable. Your best days are before you, and brokenness is not your future. There are exploits of incredible courage and breakthrough in the seasons to come that will impact our sphere of influence mightily, that your voice is establishing now as you decree and declare a thing, and as you forbid and release!

Yes, the prayers of others are powerful, but so are yours! There is nothing more powerful in your world than your voice. You, partnering with God's Word and speaking truth is not only powerful, but crucial. Your voice is a secret weapon, often the secret ingredient of breakthrough that the enemy wants silenced.

Your voice is powerful and that's why the enemy has attempted to silence you. God is weaponizing your voice and unleashing you as a faith detonator and chain breaker. Your voice is part of the solution that is unfolding as you establish the Kingdom through your decrees and prayers.

God is uncapping your potential and unleashing the faith within you to partner with Heaven and establish God's glory on the earth—specifically in your sphere of influence. Sometimes just starting something is the biggest part of the battle; so use these pages to speak out decrees and realign your faith with the God who levels mountains.

Matthew 18:18 (TPT) says, *"Receive this truth: Whatever **you** forbid on earth will be considered to be forbidden in heaven, and whatever **you** release on earth will be considered to be released in heaven."*

Let's really read that *you* is mentioned twice in that verse. Your voice is invited to partner with God in establishing His truth in and around you. This is not just an invitation however, it's a directive extended to us from the King Himself to establish this truth deep in our core. Our declarations affect the world around us, and God considered our decrees powerful enough that Heaven leans in and partners with us! It follows that as we marinate in the truth of this Scripture, it shifts from an invitation to a clarion call of compelling hope that praying this way changes things. We will no longer be satisfied with generic prayers; rather, we will desire to know the heart of God and speak forth what God is saying.

## RELEASE WHAT YOU CARRY

I often think of the story of David and Goliath, as this giant was speaking out intimidating threats and heaping fear over an entire nation. Then David comes along, a young boy really, but bold in his experience of God being with him through past life-threatening moments. He simply believed God was greater than the enemy, no matter how big the giant looked.

You probably know the story well; David, who was just taking lunch to his brothers, ended up changing a nation! Determined to see freedom, David took five stones and flung one right at Goliath, which hit the mark and Goliath fell down dead, releasing a nation from the tyranny of fear. Those stones were nothing amazing, just rocks. They were just what David had in his hand. He had built a confidence in using what was at his disposal. It wasn't until they were released and thrown in the direction of the giant, though, that they became weaponized. The stones needed to be deliberately thrown and released to take out the enemy.

Our voice is similar in that we build bold faith as we use it. Eventually, we build up a history with the Lord as each giant comes down! Declarations not spoken, are like stones not thrown at Goliath. As we open our mouths and speak, pointing our "stones" in the direction of the enemy, we weaponize our words—and remember, our fight *"is not against flesh and blood* [people], *but against the rulers, against the authorities, against the powers of this dark world and against the spiritual forces of evil in the heavenly realms"* (Ephesians 6:12 NIV). Again, our fight is not directed at people, we are decreeing truth to spiritual forces.

Picking up our weapons and purposefully throwing them looks like opening our mouths, and directing our intercession at the Goliaths that still arrogantly stand and threaten the body, the Church. But the power is in the speaking out, proclaiming out, decreeing out, and actively releasing truth as a faith-directed weapon that smashes the lies of the enemy. Release the weapon God has given you, your voice!

The stones David threw at the giant had to be thrown! Just looking at the stones or holding the stones did nothing to slay the giant. David needed to actively throw the stones with the intent of taking out Goliath, and it's the same with our decrees and intercession. The only inactive prayers are the ones we don't actually pray.

Speak it out! Release it! There is power in speaking out, releasing truth, and activating our faith to release what God is saying with *our*

YOUR VOICE IS POWERFUL

*own voice.* What are the "goliaths" in your world or nation that you are actively taking aim at with your intercession?

There is a call going out urging the inner warrior in us all to pick up our prophetic stones and throw them at the arrogance of the enemy that would dare to threaten a child of the King with intimidation. There are fields of latent destiny all around awaiting the ones whose voices will tell those dry bones to get up (Ezekiel 37), or speak to the fields of unfinished stories and say, "God isn't finished with you yet." The only decrees that aren't effective, are the ones that aren't released.

## A MIRACLE THAT SPEAKS

A lady came for prayer at the Pineapple Revival whom I have never forgotten. She walked up holding a handwritten sign that simply read, "I can't talk. I have tumors in my throat. I need a miracle. Please pray." Compassion rose up, and I prayed a simple prayer, "God, would You come heal her and give her back her voice." The woman dropped to the ground as though dead, and remained that way until the end of the meeting. We left her alone as it was obvious God was doing something.

As we were packing up at the end, ready to go home, this lady came running up to me and said, "Thank you so much for praying!" I was about to answer, when it struck me she was talking and I said with a laugh, "You can't talk?!" to which she replied, "I can now!"

Wow, we both were astounded and thanked God. She came back to the revival a few times over the next months to update us that the tumors had completely disappeared and she was totally healed. She would always tell us, "I'm still speaking!" How kind is God? He literally healed her and restored her voice! I've always thought this miracle speaks loudly to the body right now. God is giving us—His bride—our voices back. And if He has to heal some things, and remove some obstructions or obstacles to do that, He will and He is. God is amplifying the voice of the praying Church right now, and revival fire is restoring the cutting edge of the bride's decrees.

## THE NATION NOTICED

When Moses entered the tent of meeting, as he did regularly to talk to the Lord, Scripture records that the glory of the Lord was seen as a literal glory cloud that came down on the tent for the duration of their conversation. The King met with His son, the reluctant leader; and while they spoke, a literal glory cloud was seen by the whole nation. In fact, the people would know when Moses was talking to God by whether or not they could see glory over their meeting place. Wow! Something about Moses attracted the glory of God in such a way that it manifested in a "seen" way.

Moses' interactions, his conversations with the King attracted the presence of God in such a way that an entire nation knew their leader was actively seeking God. In other words, people always knew when Moses was talking with God because it was obvious, observable, and seen! Their friendship and conversations impacted the entire nation. I often think of this, and ask myself: *Are my conversations with God impacting those around me? Can people "see" the glory of God emanate from me because I've been talking to God? Does my friendship with the Holy Spirit benefit others? Does it benefit my family and city as I hear God's heart? Is God's presence observable in how I do life? Can people "see" the fruit of my friendship with God in real ways?*

"Tent of meeting" conversations are not confined to Moses' and Joshua's day. We live in a better covenant, so what Moses had is available to us as the starting place, not the ceiling. We carry His presence within us and so we are mobile "tents of meeting" with continual access to the Holy Spirit. Moses came from his cloud of glory conversations with God fresh with strategies and revelation for the nation. We too are invited to come away from meeting with the Lord and know His heart to declare, to have strategies that bring solutions. This should be our expectation.

Of course like any friendship, not every conversation contains strategies, as sometimes we are simply enjoying each other's company; but the fact remains that tent-of-meeting conversations gave Moses God's heart *to decree something and establish it,* which led a nation into destiny. This same interaction is available to us, including nation-shifting declarations and strategies from God. But let's not forget, God equally has strategies, ideas, promises, solutions, and revelation to declare over our children, our parents, our jobs, our calling, our finances, our bodies, our creative thinking...it goes on and on to include every aspect of our lives.

We are designed to desire friendship with the King, and come from our tent-of-meeting encounters with His heart to speak into our circumstances. Our friendship with God has the power to impact nations and reflect a tangible residue of His glory—so much so that at the very least those around us are impacted by the residue of God's glory from our time with Him. It's a challenging thought to think that our friendship with God should benefit our sphere of influence. God's heart revealed in our time spent with Him will naturally impact our prayer life, and result in decreeing *"a thing, and it will be established for you"* (Job 22:28 NASB).

It's from this place of intimate connection that all else flows, including the power to speak to that which needs to get in line with the Word of God.

What I've discovered is, God is more than eager to invite you into a "tent of meeting" with His heart so that you can be a voice of influence and authority decreeing on behalf of the King. He's eager to hear your thoughts and speak to all manner of situations, heart processing, and circumstances requiring divine wisdom and supernatural power. He loves to chat with you, and enjoys your company. He also invites us to know divine secrets, His thinking on a matter, and the inner thoughts of His heart (John 15:15 TPT).

This kind of friendship with the King changes everything. It changes our prayer life. It changes how we decree. For no longer are we decreeing from a place of just hope—we are declaring from a faith of knowing the heart of our King and our words carry the authority of the King backing us up. Our conversations with the Lord have now become prophetic declarations of *now* faith from the courts of Heaven. The words spoken with our own voice, our faith, are now truly edicts from the King of kings; and as any edict, it *must* be decreed.

What a great honor to steward the King's heart well; and once hearing His thoughts, be ones who will release what He is saying. I'm cautioned here to say that when our decrees come from time in His presence, it's equally important that our prayers carry not just the words, but the heart of God. It's an honor beyond honors to share in the secrets and mysteries of Heaven. May we honor His heart well and endeavor to convey this with the same heart He spoke it in.

I am often reminded in sharing God's heart to be careful to not add any "little extras" to what I am sensing Him saying and do my best to keep the message pure and true to His heart intentions. It's equally important to remember that nothing God says will ever contradict, violate, or dishonor His written Word, the Bible. His Word is not only a wise foundation, but an essential ingredient to this journey. The Bible is the written, inspired Word of God and the foundation of our faith.

It's more than words on a page—the Bible is living, active, and "God breathed" (see Hebrews 4:12 and 2 Timothy 3:16).

The Bible consists of the only words you can read that are actually *"alive and active"*:

> *For the word of God is alive and active. Sharper than any double-edged sword, it penetrates even to dividing soul and spirit, joints and marrow; it judges the thoughts and attitudes of the heart* (Hebrews 4:12 NIV).

Someone in love with the King, will also grow in love for His written Word. I will say, however, God can, and will, talk to "the world" whether they know little, lots, or none of His written Word. God doesn't check how much of the Bible people know before He starts a conversation with a hurting world.

## A CATALYTIC VISION

In 2018 I had a profound vision for the new era the Church was entering that marked me. I saw a bride dressed and ready, wielding strong and effective weapons. The weapon she used was her voice. As she spoke, I saw the dark clouds part and light pierce through the darkness. The bride was shouting, announcing, and decreeing, "On earth as it is in my Father's house" (Matthew 6:10). Her voice was not timid, reserved, or unsure—it was bold, wild, and determined. As I watched the bride use her voice as a weapon, a resolve came upon her, and with a loud shout she yelled, "ENOUGH!"

The vision then changed and I saw multitudes awaken. They came from the caves, the wilderness, from the threshing field and the mountaintops, each bore wounds and scars, but they came forth at the sound of the bride's shout. As the multitudes gathered, they turned into an army, standing to attention, immediately ready for war. I looked and saw the warrior bride, her face toward Heaven; and again I saw her raise her weapon, releasing her shout.

This time she commanded, "CHARGE!" At the intensity of her command, the army dropped to their knees and like thunder, *one voice* was raised to Heaven. Their voice, as a weapon, was sharper than any sword I'd ever seen. The bride then shouted one last impassioned command, "CHARGE, YOU WARRIORS, CHARGE YOUR WEAPONS, VICTORY IS IN SIGHT!"

> *Look at all the people coming—now is harvest time* (John 4:35 TPT).

The message of this vision is simple. It's time to charge your weapons. It's time for the bride of Christ to proclaim, "Now is the time of harvest." Your voice is writing history, your courage is shifting nations, your prayers are effecting change, your decrees are releasing breakthrough. The army of God is arising and there's a new breed of fierce warrior awakened who knows how to wield their voices as a weapon. There's an intercession revolution taking place before our eyes as the mighty decreeing bride finds her voice.

And so, *"Whatever **you** forbid on earth will be considered to be forbidden in heaven, and whatever **you** release on earth will be considered to be released in heaven."* "Wow" is probably the only worthy response. What trust God is placing in you, His friend. What very great belief He has in you. As His Kingdom ambassador, He partners with you, your words and decrees on behalf of Himself to forbid and release Heaven's edicts. Essentially, you are speaking things into being, establishing His Word and Kingdom truths, and releasing supernatural shifts that bring God-change wherever you go.

People we do not know and will never meet will benefit from the prayers we release after tent-of-meeting conversations with God. This compels me to open my mouth and speak! We have one life, and yet we have the opportunity to affect countless lives and generations to come as we decree, "Enough," and speak out "as it is in my Father's house."

I pause for a moment and acknowledge the many faithful prayers from the generations before us that we are still living in the benefit and fruit from now. Just that thought alone is enough to compel us to want to rise and decree into the days, seasons, and generations to come. Our children and those yet to be born, will live in the benefit and fruit of the prayers we decree today. This is powerful! Our prayers shape history!

You might be in circumstances that you think are small and wonder how effectual your life has been. I'm telling you, your voice is powerful and your declarations can speak to generations not yet born and affect "nations you know not" (Isaiah 55:5 NIV). Your prayers can, and are, shifting governments and laws, and calling back original destiny over families, cities, and cultural foundations.

New medical discoveries, national economic turnarounds, divine strategies for global injustices, miracle breakthroughs, inventions that affect ground-breaking change, entire nations saved in a day, and the future destiny of your own family—all this can be influenced, released, and established by those who know their God. Multitudes of souls are effected by the decrees of those who understand that their voice is powerful. And all this comes from a conversation between a King and His friend.

None of this makes sense outside of the truth that we are loved by God and cultivating a personal and authentic relationship with the Holy

Spirit. How can we know God's heart and decree God's heart without knowing God? It all starts there. And how can we stay true to the full counsel of the Lord if we do not have a love for His Word? And just knowing that it's possible to have an ongoing, current, interactive, real conversation with the King of kings who is our heavenly Father and our Friend, is compelling.

Beyond that, we need to know that our own voice carries power to shift circumstances, and God has empowered us to partner with Him in the greatest of destiny-shaping, mountain-shifting adventures. Establish that you will release what the King is saying. Your voice is powerful, anointed, and carries the authority of the King. Even in the quietness of your prayer room, bedroom, cafe table, or wherever, as you whisper His heart with seemingly no one hearing, your voice is releasing words of life that break chains and echo into eternity.

If you really believe your prayer life impacts nations and generations to come, what will you pray today? How would you pray? Would you decree with more boldness and prioritize prayer differently? If you really believe your voice is powerful, how will this affect your prayer and decrees for your family and nation?

## LET THERE BE LIGHT

God showed me just how powerful our decrees are in a wild way.

When my husband and I were ministering in Nadi, Fiji, in 2011, we were part of a revival that broke out. We watched all kinds of amazing miracles happen almost instantly, including blind eyes see, deaf ears open, many people giving their lives to God, signs and wonders like sudden strong winds that blew over all the chairs inside the church,

6-foot flames of fire seen on the stage, supernatural rain, angels singing, all kinds of healings and deliverance happening—glorious sums it up! Revival was truly breaking out.

One night I had not been feeling well and stayed home. I was alone in the bedroom and I could feel the battle in the atmosphere for continued breakthrough. I was in my room with all the lights off and it was dark, which is important to know. Suddenly, an intense "darkness" moved in. I was aware of a thick, ominous darkness and evil presence that came around our apartment and the atmosphere became like a thick fog that was trying to settle. Though it was dark in the room, I felt darkness arrive, and with it a tangible fear. It seemed every dog in the region suddenly started barking viciously as I sensed an eerie, foreboding fear.

I became immediately alert and stood to my feet to pray, knowing this was a show of force from the enemy to prevent a continued move of God. I jumped up out of bed and literally shouted, "LET THERE BE LIGHT" and began praying and marching around my bedroom. Sensing the urgency of the moment in the spirit, I shouted boldly again and decreed loudly, "LET THERE BE LIGHT!"

Immediately, the ensuite bathroom light came on by itself! My bedroom was suddenly lit up and full of light, and at the same time the evil presence and thick darkness in the atmosphere instantly dissipated. The dark that had been darker than dark receded, and strangely, every dog immediately stopped barking, too. A thick, peaceful silence descended.

I stood in my now lit-up apartment thanking God for His goodness; and honestly, a little shocked at the practical demonstration God gave me of the power of our decrees!

Commanding, "Let there be light" shifted the darkness and released the light in more ways than one that evening! I later found out that the meeting went to a new level that night too with salvation and healings flowing after much "warfare"! I've never forgotten this moment! Always remember, *your voice is powerful!* This practical sign and wonder marked me from that day. Our decrees shift things. Decree light to the darkness in your world as your prayers change things.

## THE KING'S DECREE FOR YOU

"My child, whatever you bind on earth, I consider to be bound in Heaven; and whatever you release on earth, I consider to be released in Heaven. I have given you authority to decree My voice to the world around you." —*The King*

## MY PRAYER FOR YOU

I'm praying for a new awareness of how anointed your voice is, courageous one. Contained in you are prayers that break chains in your family and release destiny in your generation. I am decreeing bold, wild, fiery, nation-shaking faith over you. Your praise is shifting the atmosphere and activating miracles in your circumstances, family, and community. I ask for more. I ask for breakthroughs that completely amaze you at how good God is. You're anointed to thrive in your life and calling, and I pray fire on your words and heart. Wherever you go, the King goes, and your prayers are evicting darkness and releasing light. I speak unparalleled glory breaking into your life, and infusing your heart and home right now. In Jesus' name, amen.

## DECREE

*My voice is powerful. I release light and evict darkness in Jesus' name. Whatever I bind on earth will be bound in Heaven. Whatever I release on earth will be released in Heaven. I am a releaser of Heaven's atmosphere and the glory of God. My voice, decrees, words, and prayers are effecting change right now. I decree that everything in my hand belongs to You, God. I will not hold back my voice; I will release it. Your authority as the King is backing me up! I will run. I will fight. I will take those giants down. I will live in victory. My voice slays the giants in my world.*

# 6

# AGREEMENT WITH GOD'S WORD RELEASES FAITH

by

*Larry Sparks*

*If you abide in Me, and My words abide in*
*you, you will ask what you desire, and it shall*
*be done for you* (John 15:7 NKJV).

In John 15:7 Jesus actually authorizes us to ask for whatever we desire, and then adds on, *"it shall be done for you."* By understanding the principle of agreeing with God's Word, we become equipped to see every impossibility come into alignment and agreement with what God says and what God wills about how a situation *should* work out. Remember, He is the Author of faith. He is the Author of the very ability that we have to speak forth words of faith, birthed by His Word, that release creative power to supernaturally transform situations. It all starts with what Jesus describes in John 15:7—abiding in His words.

I like how Bill Johnson describes this passage, "It is truly like Jesus is giving us a blank check." One has to ask, "What's the catch?" How can Jesus trust us with the offer of a blank check? When we abide in the place of closeness with God, and His words abide, rest, and remain in us, we become fit stewards to fill in the blank check with the very things that are on God's heart.

When our pursuit is God's heart, God's nature, and God's face, our prayers and declarations express this pursuit. Declaration is built on the foundation of friendship with God. It is in the context of relationship with God where His words start to take up residence in our hearts and burn their way into the very fabric of who we are. We want His realities to become manifest on the earth and His Kingdom becomes our great life quest.

Our declarations of agreement with God's Word concerning a situation or circumstance releases supernatural power to change whatever we are dealing with. It is not *our* words that have any ability to change things. Think about it. The Holy God has made a way for us mortal human beings to speak forth His immortal words and bring natural circumstances into alignment with supernatural realities. This is truly mind-blowing. Yet, this is what constantly takes place as we recognize that our mouth has become a fit resting place for the creative, transforming power of God's world-creating words.

The major difference between declaring something in faith and going down the positive confession route is that "positive confession often serves as the pretty wrapping paper on a package called denial."[1] God does not invite us to deny the challenges or impossibilities that we face; if He did, then when breakthrough was released, He would not receive the glory due His name. This is the tragedy of imbalanced positive confession theology.

I once heard of a healing evangelist who was trying to pray for a woman with a terminal disease. The woman would not acknowledge the disease, claiming that her pastor told her to not make a negative confession. The evangelist was not impressed with her line of thinking because it is a "glory thief." God gets glory when we invite Him into a situation that requires divine adjustment. When we live in denial, we are pretending that everything is okay and that by maintaining our positive confession we can simply pretend the problem away. Denying reality solves nothing and ultimately gives God *no glory* whatsoever.

When our pursuit is God's heart, God's nature, and God's face, our prayers and declarations express this pursuit.

## WORDS RELEASE SUPERNATURAL CREATIVE POWER

Jesus spoke what He first heard spoken in Heaven, and this is a fundamental key to releasing breakthrough faith through our prayers, confessions, and decrees. Jesus's words were constant "amens" of agreement to what Father God was saying. May we follow this model with our words and declarations as well. What an incredible example we have been given in our Savior who stated, "...*The words that I speak to you are spirit, and they are life*" (John 6:63 NKJV).

Declaration is a direct result of intimacy with God, and, ultimately, it is the offspring of a renewed mind. What is in our hearts and in our minds will come out of our mouths. When this happens, we become positioned to release the very life and power of God through our declarations. This is exactly what happened with Jesus. His words actually became spirit and life as He spoke out of a place of closeness with the Father.

When we start saying what we hear God saying, much like Jesus did, then our words are no longer merely verbal statements. We go beyond sentences, phrases, and grammar. When our words are in sync and in agreement with what God the Father is presently saying in Heaven, these very words take on the same quality that Jesus's did. They actually become "spirit and life." They announce realities, and go on to actually create the realities they announce. They declare a heavenly decree, and also unleash the very power to bring the decree to pass.

Somehow, the very Spirit of God was released upon the words of Jesus. The same Spirit lives inside you and me, which means that we have been invited into the same supernatural experience that Jesus lived in. His words created and destroyed. They created hope, life, healing, deliverance, and freedom while destroying torment, sickness, bondage, fear, and condemnation. Our words, in and of themselves, explain, communicate, and encourage. However, when the words of Heaven flow out of our mouth, Heaven starts transforming the earth.

This is not some pie-in-the-sky, fantasy approach to life. We need to work hard. We need to be good stewards of what we have been given. We need to make wise choices and wise decisions, and not simply think, "Well, if I confess to be debt-free, I will be!" Our positive confession will not pay the light bill or turn our marriage around in an hour. We need to take practical, biblical steps toward walking in these solutions, all the while verbally agreeing with the very heartbeat of God.

Too many faith preachers have led countless Christians into deception, promising that giving a certain amount of money or confessing a certain Bible promise so many times a day is the surefire solution to all earthly woes. No. Declaration does release supernatural solutions, but these solutions are born in the secret place of intimacy with the Father.

It is an intimate relationship with God that produces imitation. The more we live in God's Presence, the more our heart burns for His nearness. Our love for Him increases because our love for Him is always responsive—we love Him because He first loved us (see 1 John 4:19). We draw near to Him because He made the first move toward us while we were still sinners (see Romans 5:8). We change in response to who He is and how we encounter Him. We are awestruck by His beauty. We are amazed by His power. We are humbled by His holiness. We are undone by His grace and mercy.

The knowledge of God compels us to know this Glorious One who delivered us out of darkness and, through the blood of Jesus, translated us into a whole new Kingdom (see Colossians 1:13). We burn to know Him. We yearn to spend time with Him. And as the apostle Paul wrote, time in His Presence, simply beholding the One we love, transforms us into His image and likeness from one degree of glory to the next (see 2 Corinthians 3:8). The more we get to know Him, the more accurately we will be able to represent Him.

One of the ways we follow Jesus's example is through our words. In fact, our words are one of the most blatant ways that reveal our level of agreement with God's Word. In Hebrews 13:5-6 (NKJV) we read, *"...For He Himself has said, 'I will never leave you nor forsake you.' So we may boldly say: 'The Lord is my helper; I will not fear. What can man do to me?'"*

The author of Hebrews gives us a clear model on how to imitate God through our words. We simply say what God says: *"For He Himself has said... so we may boldly say...."* We declare what has *already been* said by God. I appreciate that the author added in the word "boldly." If God, the One who is faithful, true, unchanging, and perfect, says something, then we can declare it with boldness and confidence. We can

> When the words of Heaven flow out of our mouth, Heaven starts transforming the earth.

expect such words to produce fruit because they are not our words; they are God's!

Even Jesus, the very Son of God, unveiled this lifestyle of speaking *only* what God first said. Jesus's lifestyle modeled complete agreement with God, as He made it clear that He did not speak on His own authority (see John 12:49; 14:10). He said at one point, *"So whatever I speak, I am saying [exactly] what My Father has told Me to say and in accordance with His instructions"* (John 12:50 Amplified Classic). Jesus did not say whatever He felt like whenever He felt like it, expecting that the Father would bring these words to pass just because He "confessed them in faith." Jesus Christ faithfully spoke the words of the One He loved and enjoyed fellowship with—the Father.

The incredible truth is that you and I have also been summoned into this union of power and love. We enjoy fellowship with the Father because His love has called us into His Presence. It is out of this place of relationship that we speak what our Beloved has first said. This experience was not exclusively reserved for Jesus Christ alone, but is also available to all who would say yes to the Father's royal invitation. If the apostle Paul could experience this, so can you and I!

Paul wrote, *"And my speech and my preaching were not with persuasive words of human wisdom, but in demonstration of the Spirit and of power, that your faith should not be in the wisdom of men but in the power of God"* (1 Corinthians 2:4-5 NKJV). When Paul preached, natural human words did not just come out of his mouth. People were not touched by the eloquence of his speech or articulation of his oratory. When the man opened his mortal mouth, it became a conduit for the immortal Word of God. His lips become a gateway of Heaven. Paul preached God's message—the Gospel. When we declare what God is saying, our words release His supernatural power. In fact, the words *become* power. Remember what Jesus said in John 6:63 (NKJV): *"The words that I speak to you are spirit, and they are life"*? Jesus's words in our mouth carried by our speech release *God's* supernatural creative power!

## THREE KEYS TO RELEASING GOD'S POWER THROUGH DECLARATION

### 1. Stepping into Our Identity

> *Then God said, "Let Us make man in Our image, according to Our likeness; let them have dominion..."*(Genesis 1:26 NKJV).

The first key to releasing God's power through declaration is to understand that when we declare things by faith, *we are actually stepping into our identity as one fashioned in the image and likeness of Creator God.* In addition, declarations that are in agreement with the image and likeness of God release His will into circumstances that are out of order. Divine order is alignment with God's will and Heaven's culture. When we face situations in our lives that are out of order with God's perfect will, we need to step into this identity and begin declaring God's order and God's solutions. This is our starting place. Remember, we do not deny the problems we are experiencing; we are simply confronting them with our declarations of faith that are in agreement with God's Word.

Paul reminds us that our God is the One who *"gives life to the dead and calls those things which do not exist as though they did"* (Romans 4:17 NKJV). How do we respond to this dimension of God's character and nature, as a person who speaks Heaven's realities into dead places and produces life, order, and creation? We start by combining this truth with another one Paul reveals: *"Therefore be imitators of God as dear children"* (Ephesians 5:1 NKJV).

> Jesus's words in our mouth carried by our speech release God's supernatural creative power!

We are invited to imitate the One who calls things that do not exist as though they already did. The things we are "calling into existence" are not Rolex watches and sports cars. We know what we are licensed to "decree into existence" through the written Word of God combined with the revealed nature and character of God through Jesus Christ. People proof text the Bible all of the time, taking a verse here or a verse there, and somehow twist it into a passage that makes their selfish positive confessions legal. No. This cannot be. This process is much more than just knowing Bible verses and applying them to specific problems. It is actually having our hearts, minds, and words oriented to the heart, mind, and words of Father God.

## 2. Declaring Stirs Up Faith

The second key to releasing God's power through declaration is that we must recognize that *declaration stirs up the breakthrough faith within us.* We are to remember that faith is already on the inside of us. The supernatural ability to move mountains is not something special we need to climb the spiritual ladder for. Our confession does *not* give us more faith, as some people teach. It is impossible for us to receive "more faith" because we have already received the very faith of God!

We are to stir up and release what is already within us! When we start making declarations and confessions that are in agreement with the very heart, nature, and Word of God, something supernatural takes place inside of us. The potential of our faith is awakened and unlocked. It is like our words are the spark and our faith is the hay completely covered in gasoline.

Think of what happened when God initiated creation. God Himself spoke, in faith, to bring the seen out of the unseen—reality out of nothingness. A spoken decree preceded a tangible reality. In Genesis 1:3 (NKJV) we read, *"Then God said, 'Let there be light'; and there was light."* First, God *said*; *then* light came. God had faith that this thing called creation was going to work out, but there was obviously some supernatural collision that took place when words proceeded out of His mouth. They gave expression to the faith that was in His heart; God had faith in Himself and in His ability, and rightly so! We are called to model this very kind of faith in Him. This is the faith we have inherited—world-creating faith!

Now picture this: the very faith that brought creation into being actually resides on the inside of us. For us to accept the redemptive work of Jesus Christ and become a Christian, we need to have faith that our profession of faith in Christ has the power and ability to produce a specific result—*re-creating us.* We essentially believe that by making Jesus our Lord and Savior, we are being re-created in His image. Scripture says that when we are born again, we become a new creation in Christ (see 2 Corinthians 5:17). In order for us to get saved to begin with, we actually require the very faith of God that created the world, for we are placing our trust in a unique, supernatural creative process of its own. It is the re-creative process of redemption. And the good news is that if we are saved, if we are a believer in the Lord Jesus Christ, *then we have this faith already inside of us!*

## 3. Activating Kinetic Supernatural Power

The third key to releasing God's power through declaration is that when *we activate this God-sized faith through our declaration, potential*

---

*faith changes into kinetic supernatural power.* I know a lot of people who have declared and confessed Scripture until they were blue in the face—and ultimately, "blue in the faith." The main problem was not necessarily with *what* they were confessing; unfortunately, they were speaking things out of their mouths that they did not ultimately believe in their hearts.

There are people who have verbally "confessed" Christ who are still not true believers. Words matter little unless there is the vital substance of belief reinforcing those words. I could confess "I love mayonnaise" all day long, every day, for the rest of my life. But I guarantee you, this declaration would not compel me to love, like, or even tolerate the stuff because I do not believe what I am saying.

Everything in the Kingdom of God starts in the heart. Remember, our hearts believe realities about God and His Kingdom as we pursue intimacy with Him. When our hearts stand in agreement with the realities of His Kingdom, and when our mouths give voice to these truths through declaration, something powerful happens in the spirit realm. As we studied earlier, these Heaven-birthed words actually *become* life and supernatural power.

Let me illustrate this point. In science there is potential and kinetic energy. Potential energy is exactly what the name implies—it contains the potential for motion and action. I love how one website described potential energy, as "energy ready to go."[2] Faith is supernatural power that is ready to go. However, it requires action. Scripture tells us that faith without works is dead and dormant (see James 2:17-18). In fact, faith without corresponding expression is really a sham. It is poor stewardship of the supernatural gift of God living within us. It lives in this perpetual state of being *ready to go,* but sadly, it is never released and transformed into kinetic faith—supernatural power.

One such action that puts faith to work is declaration. Real-life examples of potential energy include a lawn mower filled with gasoline, a car on top of a hill, and students waiting to come home from school. All of these examples are stationary, *but* they are all ready for some catalyst to ignite them into action. Potential energy becomes *kinetic* when it is set into motion. A lawn mower requires a spark before it roars to life. In the same way, our faith is activated by the spark of the Father's words proceeding out of our mouths. God spoke, and light was.

> The very faith that brought creation into being actually resides inside us.

In my book *Breakthrough Faith,* we study a key "spark" to actually igniting this breakthrough faith. What was the catalyst that activated breakthrough faith for the four men with their paralyzed friend in Mark 2? *"Something was heard."* We have just finished exploring the vital process of what happens when this "something" is spoken aloud and declared. But what is the "something" that we need to be speaking?

There is an ancient secret that carries over from the Old Testament into the New, and that if practiced, will take the church into a whole new dimension of supernatural power and authority. The body of Christ is like that lawn mower filled to the brim with spiritual gasoline. What's missing? That vital, catalytic spark of ignition. What pushes faith out of the potential into the kinetic? What causes four guys to have such extraordinary, out-of-the-box faith that they break through a roof and lower their friend down just to get to Jesus? Testimony.

## POINT OF BREAKTHROUGH

*The secret to making Bible-based, power-producing declarations is enjoying intimate fellowship with Jesus. By being close to Him, we clearly hear His words and our passion is to imitate Him by saying what He is saying. When we speak the words of Jesus, we are speaking the words of God and His words alone release supernatural power.*

## NOTES

1. Michael J. Klassen, *Strange Fire, Holy Fire* (Minneapolis: Bethany House, 2009), 149-150.

2. "Potential & Kinetic Energy," *Energy Education,* http://www .energyeducation.tx.gov/energy/section_1/topics/potential_and_ kinetic_energy/; accessed February 11, 2014.

## RECOMMENDED READING

*Dreaming with God by Bill Johnson*

# 7

# DECREE YOUR AUTHORITY

by

*Tim Sheets*

*And I have put My words in your mouth; I have covered
you with the shadow of My hand, that I may plant the
heavens, lay the foundations of the earth, and say to
Zion, "You are My people"* (Isaiah 51:16 NKJV).

Isaiah 51:16 speaks revelation to us right now, in this day and time. However, the fullness of what God was saying to the prophet Isaiah is not going be manifested until He comes back in His millennial reign. Notice He says, *"I have put My words in your mouth."* The word for *mouth* is the Hebrew word *peh,* and it means the taste center of the body (Strong, H6310). You eat food by putting it in your mouth, chewing it up, and swallowing it. Where words are concerned, the mouth is literally the speech center of the body.

*Peh* also has a figurative meaning—the opening of the body to sound forth a command, an instruction, a prophetic word or insight, or some other communication. The mouth does this by forming and amplifying

RELEASING THE FORCE OF FAITH DECREES

words to a person, organization, congregation, nation, government, or other similar entity. God distinguishes two different realms where the words take effect, realms not talked about very much in our times but clearly emphasized by God right from the beginning—the heavens or the earth.

## PRAYERS ARE WORD SEEDS

In this verse in Isaiah 51, God talks about words sounding forth from the mouths of His sons and daughters, His heirs, into the realm of the heavens or the earth. This again emphasizes that words are seeds—word seed decrees. This also includes prayer because prayers are words of communication seeded into the heavens and into the earth. Prayer is speech to God making a request, but it is also, at times, a decree of God's promises. Prayers express confidence in God's answering abilities, or they may ask for divine intervention into a situation.

The mouth (*peh*) is the opening of the body to sound forth God's Word as seeds that grow to fullness until they are manifested in the heavens or in the earth. The mouth is, therefore, the opening through which we sow the seed of God's Word into a region. Lucifer and his kingdom seek to silence Christ's body (the church). They want our mouths closed. They don't want us to speak. Part of a demon's assignment is to shut the mouth of Christ's body. Too many in the body of Christ have fallen into that error and actually embraced it.

From the very beginning, God's original intent was for His sons and daughters, His heirs, to open their mouths and declare His words into the earth. He has put His Word in your mouth so that He may plant it in the heavens and the earth. The word for *plant* is the Hebrew word *nata,* and it means "to plant, to fix, or to set in place" (Strong, H5193). God Himself was the original Gardener, and we have inherited that job from Him as His heirs.

## GRANDPA'S GARDEN

Whenever I think about planting, I think of my grandfather Henkel. He worked at a hardware store in Waverly, Ohio, and he needed to make extra income. For probably 25 years or so, he would sell plants in the spring. He always began the process in the wintertime. I can remember, as a little kid, my grandpa sitting on the living room flipping through books of seeds and wondering aloud, "Do I want this kind of tomato plant?" "Is this the kind of seed I'm going to buy?" He would decide what kinds of seeds he was going to order.

Then, as soon as the weather broke, he would go out into what he called "hot beds," which were four or five feet wide and ten feet long, and that's where he planted everything. He would dig up all the dirt and he would burn it and mix in fertilizer and then he would go out and plant those seeds. He would cover the seeds up with plastic, and he was careful to water them and take care of them. When those plants got to maybe six to eight inches tall, he would put up his sign on the front porch: "Plants for Sale."

People came from all around Waverly, Ohio, to buy my grandpa's plants. My grandfather's seeds planted a lot of gardens in Waverly. Hundreds of people ate from them. People would come and get the little plants that he would wrap in newspaper, and they would take them home to their gardens and set them out. Of course, he saved some of the plants to set out in his own garden. He always had one of the best gardens anywhere around, and he fed his family out of that garden year round. Whatever they didn't eat they would can and save for later.

## GOD'S SPOKEN WORDS

In the beginning, God planted the stars. His word said *"be"* and it was. He set the stars, sun, and planets into place. He planted galaxies and moons with His word. He planted the heavens and He planted the earth with His word seed decrees. He told the prophet Isaiah in Isaiah 51:16 (NKJV), *"I have put My words in your mouth...that I might plant the heavens, lay the foundations of the earth."* Foundations on the earth were established according to God's decreed word. The condition of the heavens and the earth were dependent upon the word of God, His spoken word, and it still is today.

The entire universe is made to hearken to the voice of God's Word. Heaven and earth are made to respond to the voice of God's Word. Angel armies are made to respond to the voice of God's Word. Amazingly, human beings, made in God's image and likeness, are also carriers of God's voice when they are activated at the new birth. As His seed on the earth, we are to open our mouths and plant the heavens and the earth with God's Word. We are to declare the words of God into the heavens and the earth, mankind, nations, government, congregations, and people everywhere to set in place foundations for stable government and society. We are to be stewards of what God said was to be. If the foundations are not set according to God's Word, then at some point that society is going to crumble under the weight of iniquitous roots. Jesus said that such a house will not be built upon rock; it will be built upon sand, and when the storm comes it is going to fall (see Matthew 7:26).

The body of Christ is to open their mouths and plant God's Word into the earth. Like my grandfather planted produce (good seeds) into all of Waverly, we, too, are to plant God's good word seeds into our cities and regions. "I have put My words in your mouth that I might plant the heavens and the earth." Words are the seeds we plant with.

## PLANTING WORDS IN A REGION

Years ago, before I ever understood that words are seeds, I remember I was asked to go to a very small church in southern Ohio. I knew the pastor, and they had a special event going on and wanted me to come share. I don't remember what the event was, but I remember praying, "Okay, Lord. What should I share with these people?" As I prayed about it, I received revelation concerning the church ruling and reigning with Christ Jesus in this life (see Romans 5:17). I got a download of understanding and it just kept coming. Afterward I began to think, *I need to help the Lord out here.* It's something I don't attempt to do much anymore, but I said, "Lord, that's not what these people need to hear. They won't understand this. This is not even on their radar screen. This is not where they are."

God said something to me all those years ago that I have never forgotten, and it has been instruction for me concerning my apostolic calling and assignment ever since. He said, *"They will understand what I help them to understand and what I reveal to their hearts."* In other words, don't you worry about them getting fed—I will take care of that.

I have seen that over the years. I don't know how many times I have preached a sermon and somebody has come up and said, "That is exactly what I needed to hear," and proceeded to tell me what they got from the message. In the meantime, I'm thinking, "That isn't even what I said! It's not even my point!" But it was God's point to them. However many people are there, that's how many sermons you're preaching, because they're thinking about their own life situations, their own experiences, and what God is saying to them.

God said, "They'll understand what I help them understand and what I reveal to their hearts." But then He said, *"I need you to plant this word into the region."*

Now that gave me pause. I began to think, "Can I do that? Lord, can I plant a message in the heavens and the earth realm of a region? Do You really want me to plant a message, to plant doctrine from Your Word into the atmosphere of a region?"

Very clearly He said to me, "Yes. I want to grow it there. It has been requested by My people, and I need you to sow it into the region. I need you to set the foundations. I need you to lay the biblical foundation for it. It's what apostles and prophets do." I remember thinking at the time, "They do? I didn't know that." Then the Scripture came to mind that the church is built upon the foundation of the apostles and the prophets (see Ephesians 2:20). He clearly said, *"I need you to sow this into the region."*

## SEEDING THE ATMOSPHERE

I had never thought about it. It had never crossed my mind. I had never heard anybody else talk about this. But I knew a new level of understanding was being given to me, one that years later would help me with my apostolic calling. Sometimes when I am preaching, I will have the awareness that while I am talking God is going to help people understand or get something out of it, but I am also seeding the atmosphere of a region. I'm preaching a message, but I am really planting revival seeds everywhere. I'm planting God's will into the region. I am setting the foundations in the spirit realm. Sometimes I feel like I am laying a foundation in the spirit realm or into the atmosphere so that there can be productivity. I am preaching and planting the heavens. I'm preaching and planting the earth, in and around this country, for reformation and awakening.

So many times I have the awareness that God is saying, "Plant this into the region. Don't worry about it. Just plant it into the spirit realm. I want to grow it there. It's been requested by My people." Some Sunday mornings, on my way to speak, I experience understanding and begin to think, "I'm preaching this one to seed the region. I am preaching this to seed into the state. I am preaching this to seed it into the atmosphere of the United States of America." It's not always that way, but sometimes it is. I had to learn that. It is something apostles and prophets do, but it is also something all sons and daughters are supposed to do—apostles and prophets just model it.

## BUILDING A FIREWALL

This has helped me with the AwakeningNow Prayer Network, which we began in Ohio in 2008 and is spreading into the surrounding states. This network now has hundreds of churches in the region. The word from Prophet Chuck Pierce was, "Build a firewall around the entire state."

I didn't know how to build a firewall around the whole state, but in prayer Holy Spirit said, "Go to all eighty-eight counties and hold prayer assemblies." We are currently doing that—we take apostolic teams and worship teams to the prayer assemblies and we make 50 or 60 decrees into that county.

We are there to plant God's Word in the heavens and the earth of that region, and we do that with bold, faith-filled decrees of what God says. We plant prophetic words into that region. We plant that region with the will of God. We, along with the remnant believers who gather, are there to sow the atmosphere of that region with God's word seed decrees so that the rains of Heaven can come and activate them and grow them to fullness. In a sense, we are planting gardens everywhere—gardens that will be beautiful and feed and bless the people of God. Without this understanding of words as seeds or praying into the atmosphere, there is little doubt that I would be doing what I am now doing.

## PLANTING THE HEAVENS

This method of planting the heavens was also taught by Jesus. Remember that He first planted the heavens and the earth in Genesis 1. He is the Word. He planted the entire universe with word seed decrees, saying *"be"* and it was. In Matthew 6:10 (NKJV), He taught us to pray this way, *"Your kingdom come. Your will be done on earth as it is in heaven."* That's a different kind of prayer because it's not really a petition—it's a declaration. It's not a foretelling of the future—it's a commanding decree. It's calling something to be, calling something to exist. In other words, He said to declare, "Will of God, be done. Will of God, come."

When Jesus walked the earth, we see that His words caused things to happen. Wherever He went, He opened His mouth and He sounded forth decrees that brought miraculous results. In John 6:63 (NKJV) He tells us why, saying, *"The words that I speak to you are spirit, and they are life."* Understand the magnitude of that statement. When Christ spoke, when He opened His mouth and decreed, Holy Spirit moved into the atmosphere. His mouth opened the atmosphere for Holy Spirit to begin to move. Remember, Holy Spirit hovers until He hears the Word of God. When He hears the Word of God declared, He moves, just like He did upon the chaos and darkness in the beginning. Christ's mouth opened ways for the Kingdom to come. His mouth proclaimed an invitation, "Holy Spirit come. Move here."

What Jesus said produced after its kind. The superior reality of the Kingdom of God, a spiritual Kingdom that visibly affects the entire earth, began to move and transform the earth realm. The Word became a reality and produced what He decreed. The seed in the words produced it. Jesus was modeling ministry for you and me, His joint heirs.

## JOINT HEIRS

> *For you did not receive the spirit of bondage again to fear, but you received the Spirit of adoption by whom we cry out, "Abba, Father." The Spirit Himself bears witness with our spirit that we are children of God, and if children, then heirs—heirs of God and **joint heirs** with Christ, if indeed we suffer with Him, that we may also be glorified together* (Romans 8:15-17 NKJV).

*Joint heirs* is the Greek word *sygkleronomos,* and it simply means a co-heir (Strong, G4789). It is also the Greek word for *identical.* We are *identical heirs* with Christ. Because of God's grace and the free gift of righteousness through the cross, believers (born-again ones) have now been made to be identical heirs with Christ Jesus. Christ mentors those heirs (us) through the example of His earthly life, showing us how to open our mouths and sound forth Spirit-alive words. Yes, we as co-heirs can speak with the presence of the power of the Holy Spirit and can plant the heavens and the earth realms. That's staggering. That's hard to get your mind around.

When the sons and daughters of God open their mouths and decree God's Word, it can change the atmosphere of a region. Our decrees act as a catalyst that sets in motion a chain of events to bring God's Word to pass. They open the heavens so blessings can rain down, miracles can be produced, and we can receive revelation and enlightenment. Our decrees attract angel armies to ascend and descend and assist the heirs of salvation in that region (see Hebrews 1:14).

As God's heirs, as His children on the earth, we are commissioned to plant the heavens with His words, to seed them with declarations of truth. We must declare, on the basis of God's Word, the rightful rule of King Jesus over the earth, the region, and over the kingdom of darkness. We are commissioned to do it. It is well past time, but the sons and daughters of God are just waiting for Christ's return, just waiting for Him to come back. We are commanded to occupy until He comes (see Luke 19:13). We are commanded to rule and reign with Him in this life (see Romans 5:17).

We are to rule over principalities and powers, mights and dominions of darkness, binding them with superior authority just like Jesus bound them when He opened His mouth and declared that they must go. Sitting silent with closed mouths has never been an option for real heirs.

## CREATE WITH WORDS

In Isaiah 55, God tells us that His declared word becomes creative. This now starts to get very interesting. Just as God created with His words, saying *"be"* and it was, so you and I, His legitimate seeds on the earth, are restored in purpose and identity to create with our words. Our words, in alignment with God's Word when declared in faith, become creative seeds that grow and produce after their kind. Our words become creative when they are in agreement with God's Word and in alignment with Holy Spirit and His revelation to us. They open creative spheres in a region. Think about it—how could God's creative seed literally be placed in you and you not be creative in nature? The Creator seed is in us; it is our nature to be creative with our words.

> *For as the heavens are higher than the earth, so are My ways higher than your ways, and My thoughts than your thoughts. For as the rain comes down, and the snow from heaven, and do not return there, but water the earth, and make it bring forth and bud, that it may give seed to the sower and bread to the eater, so shall My word be that goes forth from My mouth; it shall not return to Me void, but it shall accomplish what I please, and it shall prosper in the thing for which I sent it* (Isaiah 55:9-11 NKJV).

> *It is the same with my word. I send it out, and it always produces fruit. It will accomplish all I want it to, and it will prosper everywhere I send it* (Isaiah 55:11 New Living Translation).

> *So will My word be which goes out of My mouth; it will not return to Me void (useless, without result), without accomplishing what I desire, and without succeeding in the matter for which I sent it* (Isaiah 55:11 Amplified Bible).

> *So will the words that come out of my mouth not come back empty-handed. They'll do the work I sent them to do, they'll*

97

*complete the assignment I gave them* (Isaiah 55:11 The Message).

## God's Promise to Us

Words are given assignments! What a promise! *"My words shall not return void." Return* is the Hebrew word *shuv,* and it means "turn around" (Strong, H7725). The promise to you and me—the born-again ones, His sons and daughters—is that the word you decree will not turn around. It cannot be reversed. It's not going to boomerang. The word for *not* is the Hebrew word *lo,* and it simply means to negate something (Strong, H3808). It's a particle of negation in the Hebrew language. It makes a positive statement negative. For example, *"I am absolutely going to do this, maybe."* That's *lo.*

Hear this: God says, "There are not going to be any maybes or I won'ts. If I said it, that's what's going to happen. If it's My word decreed, it's not going to be turned around on you. It shall not be negated. Hell will not negate it. Lucifer will not negate it. Government won't negate it. Demons won't negate it. Humanism cannot negate it. Nothing can negate it."

The word for *void* is the Hebrew word *raykawm,* and it means "empty, ineffectual, and to leak out" (Strong, H7387). God says, *"My word that My sons and daughters decree in My name does not return empty."* In other words, He is saying, "I don't give empty promises. No, they're all full. They're all effective, and they do not leak. They don't leak out." He tells Isaiah and He tells us today, *"My promises don't leak. They never return empty."*

*"It shall accomplish"* is one word in the Hebrew text and it's the word *asah,* meaning "to yield out of oneself" (Strong, H6213). That's what God does—He brings out of Himself. He creates from within Himself with His words. That's what Hebrews 11:3 (KJV) is talking about: *"Through faith we understand that the worlds were framed by the word of God, so that things which are seen were not made of things which do appear."*

The entire universe came out of God. All of creation came out of God. His words framed it. His words decreed it and described it and it produced its kind. All visible, material things were decreed by God to be. They all came out of Him as He decreed His words as seeds. Of course, if the whole universe came out of God then most certainly He can create whatever we need. How hard can that be? Our God can create any word that He speaks. No word of His is empty. When we decree God's Word, creative forces begin to flow. Even if what is needed doesn't exist, God's Word can create it.

The word *asah* also means "to become, to come to pass, to yield, or to bear" (Strong, H6213). *Asah* draws a picture of a fruit tree—it will yield whatever kind it is. The seed contains the tree that will grow from it. The fruit is also in the seed and it becomes what it is. *Asah* is also the word for *execute* or *furnish.* God's Word is furnished with power to execute and to bring that word to pass. God's Word, when decreed by His seed in alignment with His will, becomes what it is. God says it will prosper in the thing for which He sent it. *Prosper* is the Hebrew word *tsaleach,* and it means "to push forward, to break out, to be good, to be successful, or to be profitable" (Strong, H6743).

God's Word decreed becomes profitable. It breaks out of confinement. That's the way soil is pictured in the Scriptures. Soil is a confinement for the seed, but the seed breaks out of confinement to produce what it is. Word seeds break through blockages in the heavens and the earth and they are made good. They are successful. They yield and release creative abilities.

## THE POWER OF OUR DECREES

We have to understand the power in our decrees of God's Word. We almost haven't even dared to go there. Perhaps it seems too good to be true because we are accustomed to living with a negative theology that we are just downtrodden Christians waiting for Jesus to come. If that's how we think, we have not understood who we really are and who God made us to be. We have not realized that His DNA is literally transmitted into us. Our decrees, just like Jesus Christ's decrees (our identical heir), can become creative forces that break openings in the heavens or the earth for God's purpose and His plan to produce.

We have this promise: when we stand in faith and decree what God says, when we refuse to back off, when we refuse to abandon that word seed, when we water the seed with our faith, our prayers, our praise, our confession, and our steadfast trust, the seed will produce after its kind. It becomes what it is or what it describes. Never give up on a seed you plant. Never give up on God's Word. Never. Don't negate it. We are supposed to make decrees that break loose hell's grip. We can bring forth God's promises in fullness upon the earth.

As God's sons and daughters, we ought to walk this planet expecting to reap God's abundant life that His Word describes to us. We should expect:

ᚻ God's word seeds that we decree to
produce after their kind

- The word of promise to come to pass, no matter what it is
- The word seeds we sow to become fruitful and multiply
- God's Word on healing to produce the fruit of healing
- His Word that we decree on good success
  to bear the fruit of success

We should walk this planet declaring the promise and purpose of God and what His Word says. This is true in all aspects of our lives—for example, parenting. My wife, Carol, shared the following story with me that she found on Joanna Gaines' Facebook page. Joanna and Chip Gaines are the popular hosts of HGTV's *Fixer Upper* (a show I have never seen). Joanna writes:

> There's an Adonis Blue butterfly bush I planted by the girls' window almost five years ago when we were renovating the farmhouse. I wanted butterflies by the girls' windows that they could see and enjoy. I never told them about the bush and, honestly, I forgot about it over the years.
>
> This morning, I found my little Emmie sitting by her window, looking excitedly at the bush and saying, "Here she is! My little hummingbird comes every morning, Mom!" First, I didn't know she looked out for her bird every morning. Second, I forgot all about the bush and never told her if she looked out the window she would see the prettiest butterflies and hummingbirds gathered around it.
>
> It's hard not to think this is a lot like parenting. You sow seeds early on and work hard to be intentional and then, over time, you move on to new lessons and challenges. Then one day you look up and the seeds you planted in your

RELEASING THE FORCE OF FAITH DECREES

little children's hearts are now in full bloom. Be encouraged today to keep pressing in and tending to their hearts. It will be worth it. —Joanna Gaines[1]

Parenting seeds planted are still growing years later; even as an adult they are still there.

We should expect deliverance, freedom, prosperity, harvest, miracles, healings, signs, wonders, favor, strength, restoration, satisfaction, fullness, preservation, ways provided for us, help provided for us, abundance to come our way, rest for our souls, and wisdom for answers. Why? It is the seed that is in you. It's the nature of God. Remember, God's *spora* is in you. Expect the parenting seed of your Father to produce His nature. Expect His Word to produce His life everywhere. Expect bountiful gardens to come up all around you to feed and prosper your life. Words are seeds. They grow and they become after their kind.

Prophet Chuck Pierce recently released this prophetic word, which illustrates the importance of your words as seeds:

Many seeds have been planted, and many seeds are now waiting for a chance in the atmosphere so they can sprout. These seeds are not lying desolate but are waiting for an atmosphere of refreshing and rejoicing that will cause them to break forth. This is a time I'm sending out those who will go to those places where seeds are sown, and from the seeds being sown they will open a portal so the rain of My Spirit can come. Then they will harvest and bring back to the storehouse what needs to be brought back. Seeds are waiting. Your portal will carry the water to bring forth the harvest of grain that has fallen into the earth for a season of death. From the death of past fields a great harvest will come!

Amen!

## NOTE

1. Joanna Gaines' Facebook page, https://www.facebook.com/JoannaStevensGaines/?fref=nf; March 15, 2017.

# 8

# RELEASING PRAYERS OF POWER

by

*Tommy and Miriam Evans*

Daily declarations have changed everything for us. Once we realized the biblical principle of speaking over our destinies, we began to partner with what God says about us in His Word by making declarations over ourselves. As we did this, we noticed a dramatic shift. A positive change took place in our earthly perspectives, one that unlocked Heaven's power over our lives. Worldly circumstances no longer limited Heaven's activity over our lives (see Colossians 3:2). The shift came from within us. We believe that declaring biblical truths over your life will release the power of transformation.

This powerful transformation is the result of some fascinating keys found in Scripture. We believe Romans 12:2 (NKJV) is one of those keys: *"...be transformed by the renewing of your mind...."* According to Scripture, this is the first step to discerning God's will for our lives.

Transformation begins with the way we think, and how we think influences the way we speak. Luke 6:45 (NKJV) says, *"...For out of the abundance of the heart his mouth speaks."* The words we speak flow from

RELEASING THE FORCE OF FAITH DECREES

what we believe. What we believe affects the words we speak, thus creating an interesting ellipse. Our thoughts and words work so closely together it is sometimes difficult to decipher which influence comes first. For that reason, the Bible tells us that we must guard our hearts because our heart's status effects life issues (see Proverbs 4:23). It may be safe to conclude our thought life determines who we are and the decisions we make.

The Hebrew word for *heart* is *levav,* which includes thoughts, will, discernment, and affections. Proverbs 23:7 tells us that as a man believes in his heart, so is he.

Studying the Bible helped us realize the truth concerning our thought life. We found that our thoughts began to change when we chose to speak positively, regardless of our feelings. Speaking what God says about us is a game-changer. Declaring God's truth, despite life's circumstances, changes everything. Jesus demonstrates this beautifully in the gospel of Luke.

In Luke 4, we find a powerful story telling when Jesus made a public declaration of what the Father said about Him.

In the synagogue on the Sabbath, Jesus picked up the scroll of Isaiah 61 and read aloud a prophecy about the coming Messiah. Jesus knew He was reading a prophecy about Himself among the people of His hometown. This story demonstrates the power of declaration. The people who were all too familiar with this carpenter's son were stunned at the words Jesus spoke, as great authority shifted the atmosphere. He did not wait for people to recognize He was the Son of God before He declared who He was. Therefore, Jesus powerfully declared, *"The Spirit of the Lord is upon me, and he has anointed me to be hope for the poor, healing for the brokenhearted, and new eyes for the blind, and to preach to prisoners, 'You are set free!'"* (Luke 4:18 TPT).

In Luke 4, we read that Jesus made this declaration after a defining moment in the wilderness. Jesus knew His identity amid the trial. He came out of the wilderness *"armed with the Holy Spirit's power"* (Luke 4:14 TPT). Upon leaving the wilderness, the Holy Spirit led Jesus to His hometown synagogue to speak His identity audibly. Jesus declared what the heavenly Father said about Him through the prophet Isaiah. Isaiah's prophecy, found in Isaiah 61, was spoken hundreds of years before this moment took place. Luke 4:21 says that Jesus concluded his public declaration of Isaiah 61 by saying, *"Today this Scripture is fulfilled in your hearing."*

Through the prophet Isaiah, God made a promise of the coming Messiah, His Son, Jesus Christ. As Jesus declared this promise, God fulfilled the promise. When we declare God's promises over our lives, we create a partnership with God to see these promises fulfilled. When we speak God's promises, we create a sound of completion. Genesis 1 says that when God spoke, *"Let there be light,"* all chaotic circumstances came into order. We see a fulfillment of miracles throughout Scripture as Jesus spoke. Like Jesus, we can shape our future with our words. Jesus is and always will be the perfect prototype for humanity. Throughout the Bible, Jesus declared the Father's words to see a fulfillment. It would behoove us to do the same.

May you be filled with the Holy Spirit as you daily read and declare God's Word over your life. May you be empowered to believe what God says about you. May this be a catalyst to unlock Heaven's power over your life. May every promise be fulfilled in your hearing.

## RELEASING PRAYERS OF POWER

What God says about you:

> *...for tremendous power is released through the passionate, heartfelt prayer of a godly believer!* (James 5:16 TPT)

> *You will also declare a thing, and it will be established for you; so light will shine on your ways* (Job 22:28 NKJV).

Your prayers carry creative power! Jesus gave His disciples a prayer model that includes, *"On earth as it is in heaven"* (Matthew 6:10). Heaven is our focus for all prayer. We are asking God's world to invade ours according to the order of Heaven. We believe today that as you open your heart to these truths you will be activated to a new level of power in your personal prayer life. Now activate this truth by speaking the following declarations over your life. Much Love!

## Declarations:

James 5:16; Job 20:28; John 15:16; Ephesians 2:6; Mark 11:26

---

- ⵏ "Because I have been given a seat of power in the heavenly realm through Christ, my prayers are powerful and effective."

- ⵏ "Today I believe as I pray according to Your will, I will receive what I am asking for."

- ⵏ "When I pray, the Kingdom is unlocked, and Heaven is opened to invade impossible situations, turning things around for my good and those I love, in Jesus' name."

- "I know in my heart that God hears my prayers, and He will answer me."
- "My prayers release the Kingdom and declare God's perfect will in the earth."

## Prayer:

*"Lord Jesus, thank You for giving up Your life so that I have access to pray and commune with You. I love You so much. Amen."*

## GOD'S PROMISES

What God says about you:

*...There has not failed one word of all His [God's] good promise...* (1 Kings 8:56 NKJV).

*Not one promise from God is empty of power. Nothing is impossible with God!* (Luke 1:37 TPT)

Wow! What powerful promises are found in God's Word! When God gives us a promise, it never fails! Every promise God has made to us carries fulfillment power! Get ready to receive your promise! Now activate this truth by speaking these declarations over your life. Much Love!

## Declarations:

Ephesians 3:20; 1 Kings 8:56; Luke 1:37;
Numbers 23:19; Psalm 119:89

---

- "I trust all of Your promises for me because there is divine power in them to be fulfilled."

- "Every promise You have ever made to me will be fulfilled in my life and in the lives of those I love, in Jesus' name."

- "As I hold on to what is true, I give myself permission to exaggerate Your goodness over me because I know You are faithful."

- "You are the Lord who exceeds my wildest imagination and fulfills my wildest dreams. Today I declare that I am one step closer to my dreams being realized beyond imagination!"

- "Nothing is impossible with God; therefore, I will see my promises come to pass."

## Prayer:

*"Lord, thank You that You truly are the God of promises. I make a promise to You that today I will eagerly anticipate Your goodness being made manifest. I love You, Lord. Amen."*

## WALKING IN THE MIRACULOUS

What God says about you:

*And these miraculous signs will accompany those who believe: They will drive out demons in the power of my name. They will speak in tongues. They will be supernaturally protected from snakes and from drinking anything poisonous. And they will lay hands on the sick and heal them* (Mark 16:17-18 TPT).

Did you know that Jesus lived a miracle life? His whole life was a miracle! Jesus said, *"As the Father has sent Me, I also send you"* (John 20:21 NKJV). That's great news! Jesus has sent you and me to live a life of the miraculous! Now is the time for you to step into the fullness of your inheritance! Now activate this truth by speaking these declarations over your life. Much Love!

## Declarations:

Mark 16:17-18; Matthew 10:7-8; Acts 5:12; Acts 19:11-12

- ⵟ "Because I believe in Jesus, I live a life of the miraculous with signs and wonders following me."
- ⵟ "Like Jesus, I live a miracle life."
- ⵟ "God releases a flow of extraordinary miracles through my hands, through my words, and through my life."
- ⵟ "When I see an impossible situation, I run to it, knowing that God will bring about a miracle."
- ⵟ "Creative miracles are a normal occurrence for me because I am a child of God."
- ⵟ "Miracles are normal for me, in Jesus' name!"

## Prayer:

*"Lord, I am so grateful that You would choose me to live a life of the miraculous. May every miracle in my life bring glory and honor to Your name. Amen."*

## DIVINE HEALING FOR YOURSELF

What God says about you:

*...For I am the Lord who heals you* (Exodus 15:26 NKJV).

*He sent His word and healed them...* (Psalm 107:20 NKJV).

*...and by His stripes we are healed* (Isaiah 53:5 NKJV).

Did you know that Jesus died on the cross not only for your eternal salvation, but also for your deliverance and divine healing? The biblical word for *salvation* is *sozo*, which means "healed, saved, and delivered." Jesus paid a price so you can be healed! According to the Bible it is 100 percent God's will for you to walk in divine health. Divine healing is your inheritance! Now activate this truth by speaking these declarations over your life. Much Love!

## Declarations:

Exodus 15:16; Psalm 107:20; Isaiah 53:5; Acts 10:38; Luke 5:13; Romans 8:11; Luke 4:40

⸶ "Because Jesus healed everyone who came to Him, I come to Him and choose today to walk in divine health by the power of His name."

⸶ "I speak to my body and command it to line up according to the order of God's will that I am healed by the stripes of Jesus."

⸶ "Because Jesus went to the cross for my healing, I declare that I am healed."

⸶ "Sickness, pain, and disease have no authority over my body, in Jesus' name."

⸶ "The Spirit of resurrection power lives in me and brings life to my mortal being."

⸶ "You sent forth Your Word for me so that I can now stand in perfect health."

**Prayer:**

*"Lord, thank You for Your healing power. I believe that You died on the cross not only for my salvation, but also my healing. I agree that I am healed in Jesus' name according to Your Word. Amen."*

## RELEASING HEALING POWER

What God says about you:

*Empower us, as your servants, to speak the word of God freely and courageously. Stretch out your hand of power through us to heal, and to move in signs and wonders by the name of your holy Son, Jesus!* (Acts 4:29-30 TPT)

*Jesus repeated his greeting, "Peace to you!" And he told them, "Just as the Father has sent me, I'm now sending you"* (John 20:21 TPT).

*And these signs will follow those who believe: In My name they will cast out demons; they will speak with new tongues; they will take up serpents; and if they drink anything deadly, it will by no means hurt them; they will lay hands on the sick, and they will recover* (Mark 16:17-18 NKJV).

According to the Bible, you carry healing power! Christ has not only given you authority and permission to lay hands on the sick, but He has given each one of us a mandate to heal in His name. There is healing power in your hands and in your mouth! Now activate this truth by speaking these declarations over your life. Much Love!

## Declarations:

Acts 4:29-30; Acts 4:12-16; Matthew 10:7-8; Mark 16:17-18; Matthew 4:23-24; Luke 4:40; Acts 10:38; James 5:15

⸸ "Like Jesus, I am anointed with the Holy Spirit. Because I know God is with me, I choose today to do good by healing the sick and setting free those who are oppressed by the devil."

- "I have been commissioned by Jesus to heal the sick and cast out demons."

- "When I lay hands on the sick, they will recover in Jesus' name."

- "My hands and my words carry healing power."

- "Because Jesus lives inside me, I have authority to release healing to my family, friends, and community."

**Prayer:**

> *"Lord, thank You for anointing me with Your Spirit to bring healing to others. May the healing power of Jesus be displayed in my life and bring You glory on earth. Amen."*

## GOD ENCOUNTERS

What God says about you:

> *...I will pour out My Spirit on all flesh; your sons and your daughters shall prophesy, your old men shall dream dreams, your young men shall see visions* (Joel 2:28 NKJV).

> *Then suddenly, after I wrote down these messages, I saw a portal open into the heavenly realm, and the same trumpet-voice I heard speaking with me at the beginning said, "Ascend into this realm! I want to reveal to you what must happen after this"* (Revelation 4:1 TPT).

Did you know that by design you were engineered to encounter God? God encounters are part of your inheritance as a believer! The Bible was not given to us just to make us smarter and brighter. The reason the Bible has been given to us was to lead us into a divine encounter with its Author! Jesus wants you to encounter Him! This is the good news of the Kingdom! Now activate this truth by speaking these declarations over your life. Much Love!

## Declarations:

> Joel 2:28; Habakkuk 2:2-3; Amos 3:7; Numbers 12:6;
> 2 Corinthians 12:4; 1 Corinthians 2:10;
> Revelation 4:1-2; Matthew 17; book of Acts

- ✝ "I consistently have dreams, visions, and prophetic encounters."
- ✝ "Heavenly encounters, angelic visitations, and spiritual happenings are normal to me and are part of my inheritance as a child of God."
- ✝ "Like Jesus and His disciples, I carry an open heaven where angels ascend and descend on my life carrying fresh revelation, strength, and assignments."
- ✝ "The Holy Spirit is my guide with all heavenly encounters and teaches me how to navigate through them."

## Prayer:

*"Thank You, Holy Spirit, that You search the deepest mysteries of God and make them known to me. Lord,*

*I choose today to step into divine encounters through faith. I am so thankful that I have the privilege to discover all that You have for me. I love You. Amen."*

## LIVING IN CONTAGIOUS JOY

What God says about you:

> *For the kingdom of God is not a matter of rules about food and drink, but is in the realm of the Holy Spirit, filled with righteousness, peace, and joy* (Romans 14:17 TPT).

> *...in Your presence there is fullness of joy; at Your right hand are pleasures forevermore* (Psalm 16:11 NKJV).

> *He who sits in the heavens shall laugh...* (Psalm 2:4 NKJV).

According to Romans 14:17, joy is one third of the Kingdom! When my children were babies, any time I would reach down and get in their face they would always smile. In the Bible, the meaning for the word *presence* is "face." So when Psalm 16:11 states, *"in Your presence is fullness of joy,"* it's saying, "In God's *face* there is fullness of joy." When we get in our heavenly Father's face, it puts a smile on ours! Now activate this truth by speaking these declarations over your life. Much Love!

## Declarations:

Romans 14:17; Nehemiah 8:10; Psalm 2:4;
Hebrews 1:9; Proverbs 17:22

✝ "Because I am filled with the Spirit of God,
I am filled with contagious joy."

✝ "I laugh hysterically at every lie of the devil
because I know that God has my back!"

✝ "Like Jesus, I am anointed with the oil of
joy that is transferable to others."

✝ "I walk in an abundance of joy that brings healing
to my entire being—spirit, soul, and body."

✝ "Joy through laughter is a weapon that God has
equipped me with for any challenge that I might face."

✝ "I am filled today with God's joy that brings
healing to my body and gladness to my heart."

## Prayer:

*"Lord, thank You for the gift of joy. Today I choose
to let You fill me again with great joy. Amen."*

## Living in the Holy Spirit

What God says about you:

*And I will ask the Father and he will give you another Savior, the Holy Spirit of Truth, who will be to you a friend just like me—and he will never leave you. The world won't receive him because they can't see him or know him. But you know him intimately because he will make his home in you and will live inside you* (John 14:16-17 TPT).

*If the Spirit is the source of our life, we must also allow the Spirit to direct every aspect of our lives* (Galatians 5:25 TPT).

Did you know that because of Jesus you no longer live in your old sin nature, but you now live in the Spirit? When you received Jesus, you became one in spirit with Him. You have eternal access to His thoughts, affections, and fellowship. You have permission to enjoy a beautiful journey with the Holy Spirit! Now activate this truth by speaking these declarations over your life. Much Love!

## Declarations:

1 Corinthians 6:17; Galatians 5:25; Romans 8:9;
John 14:16-17; John 7

---

- "I believe in my heart that the Holy Spirit has come to me so that I may have intimate fellowship with Him."
- "I speak to my body, soul, and spirit and say, 'You are not dominated by the flesh—you are led by the impulses of the Holy Spirit.'"

---

⳨ "Today I declare that no other spirit shall rule over me
but the empowering presence of the Holy Spirit."

⳨ "Because of Jesus, I have been unified forever
with the Holy Spirit who never leaves me."

⳨ "I declare that my love for the Holy Spirit
grows deeper and deeper every day."

⳨ "I am a friend of the Holy Spirit. My love for
Him grows deeper and wider every day."

**Prayer:**

*"Holy Spirit, thank You for coming to be my Helper,
Teacher, Comforter, and Friend. I cannot wait to spend
the rest of my days with You. I love You deeply. Amen."*

## VICTORIOUS LIVING

What God says about me:

*Now thanks be to God who always leads us in triumph in
Christ, and through us diffuses the fragrance of His knowledge
in every place* (2 Corinthians 2:14 NKJV).

*And the Lord said to Joshua, "Do not fear them, for I have
delivered them into your hand..."* (Joshua 10:8 NKJV).

*The horse is prepared for the day of battle, but deliverance is of
the Lord* (Proverbs 21:31 NKJV).

*For the Lord alone is my Savior. What a feast of favor and bliss he gives his people!* (Psalm 3:8 TPT)

Did you know that God never leads you to a place where you will fail? When God leads us, the result will always be victory! His grace and love over your life set you up to be victorious in every situation! Now activate this truth by speaking these declarations over your life. Much Love!

## Declarations:

2 Corinthians 2:14; Joshua 10:8; Proverbs 21:31; Psalm 3:8

- "I am wearing today's perfume of victory!"
- "Like Jesus, I am victorious."
- "I talk and act like a winner because I am a winner!"
- "I declare, since God is on my side, nothing can stand in my way to victory!"
- "When others get around me, they smell the fragrance of victory and are inspired to step into victory with me!"
- "Every enemy that tries to stop me, hinder me, or crush me will be defeated because God has delivered them into my hand!"

## Prayer:

*"Lord, thank You that the shed blood of Jesus makes me victorious in every situation. Because You are on my side, I cannot be defeated. Amen."*

## KINGDOM WARFARE

What God says about you:

*For the weapons of our warfare are not carnal but mighty in God for pulling down strongholds, casting down arguments and every high thing that exalts itself against the knowledge of God, bringing every thought into captivity to the obedience of Christ* (2 Corinthians 10:4-5 NKJV).

*He raised us up with Christ the exalted One, and we ascended with him into the glorious perfection and authority of the heavenly realm, for we are now co-seated as one with Christ!* (Ephesians 2:6 TPT)

Did you know that you are co-seated with Christ? We are called to war against our enemies from Heaven to earth, not from earth toward Heaven. We have an aerial view! We have a victory perspective! Because we are sitting next to Him, He speaks to our hearts and gives us words to declare that bring about Kingdom victory! Now activate the truth of God's Word by speaking these declarations over your life. Much Love!

## Declarations:

Ephesians 6; Ephesians 1:19-22;
2 Corinthians 10:3-5; Ephesians 2:6; Colossians 1

⅄ "God is on my side; therefore, I cannot
be defeated, in Jesus' name!"

- "I am seated with Christ in heavenly places; therefore, I say to anxiety, fear, torment, heaviness, and depression to get under my feet, in Jesus' name!"

- "I am co-seated with Christ far above every seat of power, realm of government, principality, and authority in the heavenly realm."

- "I declare that strongholds are pulled down and dismantled because my mind has been renewed to take captive lies from the enemy."

- "I command my soul to never be impressed by what the enemy is doing. Today I refine my focus to see and hear the good things that God is doing."

## Prayer:

*"Lord, thank You that my weapons are mighty in God! You have equipped me for every good work. Thank You for giving me the victory! Amen."*

## WORDS OF LIFE

What God says about you:

*Simon Peter replied, "Lord, to whom would we go? You have the words that give eternal life"* (John 6:68 NLT).

*But if you live in life-union with me and if my words live pow-*
*erfully within you—then you can ask whatever you desire and*
*it will be done* (John 15:7 TPT).

*So also will be the word that I speak; it does not return to me*
*unfulfilled. My word performs my purpose and fulfills the mis-*
*sion I sent it out to accomplish* (Isaiah 55:11 TPT).

*Then God said, "Let there be light," and there was light*
(Genesis 1:3 NLT).

The Bible exists by the *Word* of God, and everything exists from His spoken word (see John 1:1-3). Jesus's words carry life because He is life. Throughout Scripture, we can observe that words matter. Being united with Christ includes being connected with His written and spoken word daily. From this place of oneness with Christ, His life-giving words will be in us. When we speak what He says, we co-labor with Him to create life, hope, and miracles into situations. Now activate the truth of God's Word by saying these declarations over your life. Much Love!

## Declarations:

John 12:9-12; John 15; Genesis 1; John 1; Proverbs
18:21; Isaiah 55:11; Matthew 21:21; Hebrews 1:3

---

⸸ "I create with my words."

⸸ "When I speak God's Word, chaos comes into order."

⸸ "My words create miracles that glorify Jesus."

⸸ "My words contain life-giving power."

❧ "My words navigate my life; therefore, I choose to speak words that positively change the course of my life."

❧ "The Father's words over me are kind, gentle, and forgiving of my mistakes; now, I give those same words to others."

## Prayer:

*"Heavenly Father, thank You for sending Jesus, who is Your living Word. Help me to remain in life-union with You. Holy Spirit, fill me with the love, the power, and the words of Jesus. Fill my mouth with words that bring life to myself, my family, and my loved ones. I believe that You will transform me with Your words toward me. Thank You for Your merciful words that birth miracles. Amen."*

## LIVING LIKE JESUS

What God says about you:

*The Son is the dazzling radiance of God's splendor, the exact expression of God's true nature—his mirror image! He holds the universe together and expands it by the mighty power of his spoken word. He accomplished for us the complete cleansing of sins, and then took his seat on the highest throne at the right hand of the majestic One* (Hebrews 1:3 TPT).

*By living in God, love has been brought to its full expression in us so that we may fearlessly face the day of judgment, because all that Jesus now is, so are we in this world* (1 John 4:17 TPT).

*I want you to pattern your lives after me, just as I pattern mine after Christ* (1 Corinthians 11:1 TPT).

Living like Jesus is more than a smile and a good mood. Living like Jesus is living a life of the miraculous that serves humanity. It is living a life that brings glory to the Father! When we read transformation stories in the Bible, His Word promises that we have permission to do the same. Jesus fulfills the will of God. Doing what Jesus did here on earth mirrors God's will (see Hebrews 1:3). Everything that Jesus is *now* is what we have access to be on this earth. Now activate the truth of God's Word by saying these declarations over your life. Much Love!

## Declarations:

John 15; John 17:10; Acts 10:38;
Mark 16:17-18; Romans 8:11; Romans 8:17

ᛉ "All that Jesus did on this earth, I can do because He lives in me!"

ᛉ "Jesus is my perfect example, and I have the power of the Holy Spirit to help me live like Him."

ᛉ "God gives me creative ways to do good for others."

ᛉ "My actions transform the world around me."

ᛉ "I have the same Spirit of Jesus; therefore, I can expect to have miracles, signs, and wonders follow me."

**Prayer:**

*"Jesus, thank You for going to the cross for me so that I could have all that is Yours. I give You my past with all its failures and disappointments. I ask that You fill me with the **same** Spirit who brings resurrection life. Holy Spirit, I need You to live a life like Jesus. Amen."*

## JESUS MAKES ME ENOUGH

What God says about you:

*She gives out revelation-truth to feed others. She is like a trading ship bringing divine supplies from the merchant* (Proverbs 31:14 TPT).

*Never doubt God's mighty power to work in you and accomplish all this. He will achieve infinitely more than your greatest request, your most unbelievable dream, and exceed your wildest imagination! He will outdo them all, for his miraculous power constantly energizes you* (Ephesians 3:20 TPT).

*And you did not receive the "spirit of religious duty," leading you back into the fear of never being good enough. But you have received the "Spirit of full acceptance," enfolding you into the family of God. And you will never feel orphaned, for as he rises up within us, our spirits join him in saying the words of tender affection, "Beloved Father!"* (Romans 8:15 TPT).

Like many, I have had my fair share of overcoming feelings of inadequacy. The fear of not being enough blocks us from walking in abundant life. Jesus fills in all our gaps and makes our ordinary extraordinary! He desires to partner with us to fulfill our greatest dreams. Resting in the Father's acceptance is part of the adoption process. Let His love qualify you. Now activate the truth of God's Word by saying these declarations over your life. Much Love!

## Declarations:

Romans 8:17; Romans 8:14-16; Proverbs 31:14;
Exodus 4:10-12; Amos 7; Judges 6:15-16

---

✝ "I am capable, and I have what it takes to succeed."

✝ "I don't wait for others to recognize my
gifting before I act in faith."

✝ "I am adopted and accepted by my heavenly Father."

✝ "God's love qualifies me."

✝ "Jesus gives me revelation truth, and
I bring miracles to others."

✝ "Because of what Jesus paid for on the cross, I
bring supernatural supplies from Heaven."

## Prayer:

*"Father, thank You for adopting me into Your family.
Thank You, Holy Spirit, for making God's fatherhood
real to me. Father, I believe that You gave Your Son so I*

*could inherit all Your treasures, including the greatest miracle of salvation. I believe I can bring miracles and truth to those in need. Today I give You my yes. Amen."*

## ARISE AND SHINE

What God says about you:

> *Arise, shine; for your light has come! And the glory of the Lord is risen upon you. For behold, the darkness shall cover the earth, and deep darkness the people; but the Lord will arise over you, and His glory will be seen upon you. The Gentiles shall come to your light, and kings to the brightness of your rising* (Isaiah 60:1-3 NKJV).

> *You are the light of the world. A city that is set on a hill cannot be hidden. Nor do they light a lamp and put it under a basket, but on a lampstand, and it gives light to all who are in the house. Let your light so shine before men, that they may see your good works and glorify your Father in heaven* (Matthew 5:14-16 NKJV).

Did you know that you were created to shine brightly for the King of Glory? Jesus came as the light of the world, and then He passed the baton off to you and me, then said, *"You are the light of the world"* (Matthew 5:14). You and I have become the very image of the One and only Jesus Christ! We have become His exact representation! We are image bearers of light in the darkness! Now is the time for you to arise and shine to a lost and dying world! Now activate this truth by declaring these biblically based declarations over your life. Much Love to you!

## Declarations:

Matthew 5:14-16; Isaiah 60; Matthew 10:7-8; Matthew 28; Acts 1:8; Mark 16:15; Hebrews 1:1-3; Colossians 1

- "Today I will arise and shine, reflecting the beauty of Jesus everywhere I go."
- "I am salt and light to the world. My life causes those around me to become hungry for God."
- "My life is the express image of Jesus."
- "The glory of God shall be seen upon me and nations shall come to the light that I carry."

## Prayer:

*"Lord Jesus, thank You for putting Your light and life in me. Help me to shine brightly and reflect Your beauty. I love You. Amen."*

Your prayers carry creative power! Jesus gave His disciples a prayer model that includes, *"On earth as it is in heaven"* (Matthew 6:10 NKJV). Heaven is our focus for all prayer. We are asking God's world to invade ours according to the order of Heaven. We believe today that as you open your heart to these truths you will be activated to a new level of power in your personal prayer life. Now activate this truth by speaking these declarations over your life. Much Love!

## Declarations:

James 5:16; Job 20:28; John 15:16; Ephesians 2:6; Mark 11:26

---

- ⸹ "Because I have been given a seat of power in the heavenly realm through Christ, my prayers are powerful and effective."

- ⸹ "Today I believe as I pray according to Your will, I will receive what I am asking for."

- ⸹ "When I pray, the Kingdom is unlocked, and Heaven is opened to invade impossible situations, turning things around for my good and those I love, in Jesus' name."

- ⸹ "I know in my heart that God hears my prayers, and He will answer me."

- ⸹ "My prayers release the Kingdom and declare God's perfect will on earth."

## Prayer:

*"Lord Jesus, thank You for giving up Your life so that I have access to pray and commune with You. I love You so much. Amen."*

9

# OPERATING AS A JUDGE

by

*Robert Henderson*

**B**efore we move fully into prayer, decrees, and declarations in the Courts of Heaven, we should understand this realm from the position of a judge. Most Christians would say God is the Judge. We might, however, be surprised to find that God would allow us to operate as "judges" in the realm of the spirit as well. In fact, the whole idea of decrees and declarations emerges from this concept. Judges are those whose words change the course of events. Judges' decrees, declarations, and verdicts set things in motion that wouldn't otherwise happen. We actually can be granted this role from which these statements can be made!

In Job 22:27-28 (NKJV), we see this idea:

> *You will make your prayer to Him, He will hear you, and you will pay your vows. You will also declare a thing, and it will be established for you; so light will shine on your ways.*

This Scripture passage actually says we can declare something and see it established. In other words, our words in the spirit realm cause something to happen in the natural realm. This can be because we are sitting as judges in these dimensions. When someone challenged my idea about us becoming judges, I reminded the person that God actually put a book in the Bible called "Judges." It chronicles the life of both men and women who functioned as judges to set justice in place. In fact, judges were God's first choice to create and sustain order in society. Only after the people cried for a "king" did God grant them one. Before this, there were judges. We find in 1 Samuel 8:19-22 (NKJV) God giving in and granting them a king instead of judges:

> *Nevertheless the people refused to obey the voice of Samuel; and they said, "No, but we will have a king over us, that we also may be like all the nations, and that our king may judge us and go out before us and fight our battles." And Samuel heard all the words of the people, and he repeated them in the hearing of the Lord. So the Lord said to Samuel, "Heed their voice, and make them a king." And Samuel said to the men of Israel, "Every man go to his city."*

Even though Samuel warned them from God what would happen if they had a king, they still demanded it. I am showing you this simply to make the point that this wasn't God's ideal. God's perfect situation was judges who were before kings. In fact, when things became corrupt in Israel, God's solution was to restore judges. Isaiah 1:26 (NKJV) shows that when Jerusalem was full of wickedness and sin, God's fix was reinstituting judges:

> *I will restore your judges as at the first, and your counselors as at the beginning. Afterward you shall be called the city of righteousness, the faithful city.*

God said when there were judges and counselors again, the city would be known as a righteous and faithful place. This is the power of judges.

Righteous judges can bring order and peace back into place. This is true in the natural but also in the spirit realm. We need righteous and just judges in the natural, but we also need them in the spirit to set things in divine order through decrees and declarations.

Jesus actually spoke of His apostles operating as judges. In Luke 22:28-30 (NKJV), we see Jesus promising His apostles positions as judges:

> *But you are those who have continued with Me in My trials. And I bestow upon you a kingdom, just as My Father bestowed one upon Me, that you may eat and drink at My table in My kingdom, and sit on thrones judging the twelve tribes of Israel.*

I personally do not believe this was just in the afterlife; I believe Jesus was speaking in the spiritual dimension right now. In other words, He was promising them that because of their faithfulness, they would operate as judges. This is what Peter did in Acts 5:1-5 (NKJV) when he judged Ananias and then later Sapphira:

> *But a certain man named Ananias, with Sapphira his wife, sold a possession. And he kept back part of the proceeds, his wife also being aware of it, and brought a certain part and laid it at the apostles' feet. But Peter said, "Ananias, why has Satan filled your heart to lie to the Holy Spirit and keep back part of the price of the land for yourself? While it remained, was it not your own? And after it was sold, was it not in your own control? Why have you conceived this thing in your heart? You have not lied to men but to God." Then Ananias, hearing these words, fell down and breathed his last. So great fear came upon all those who heard these things.*

Peter spoke judgment upon them because of their deception and sin. The result was that fear of the Lord came not just upon the church, but also upon the culture. Ananias and his wife Sapphira lied to the Holy Spirit. This was obviously a heinous thing to do. This should make us more aware of how we must treat the Holy Spirit. Their sin of lying to the Holy Spirit caused God to judge them. He used Peter, however, to render this judgment upon them.

My reason for speaking of this is to clarify that God grants us a position as judges. Even though we might consider judgment "negative," the real reason for judgment is to set in place justice and divine order. God told the prophet Jeremiah that his ministry would be to destroy and then build. This statement refers to the ability to judge. Jeremiah 1:10 (NKJV) speaks of the authority granted Jeremiah to deal with kingdoms. God says:

> See, I have this day set you over the nations and over the kingdoms, to root out and to pull down, to destroy and to throw down, to build and to plant.

Jeremiah would be allowed to render judgments in the spirit that removed evil from nations and kingdoms. He would also be allowed to render judgments that built and established nations. Anything that happens in the natural first occurred in the spirit. When judges take their place in the spirit realm, divine order can come in the natural. As judges in the realm of the spirit, we are setting things in order in agreement with God's justice. In 1 Corinthians 2:15 (NKJV) we are told that those who are spiritual "judge" all things: *"But he who is spiritual judges all things, yet he himself is rightly judged by no one."*

The words *judges* and *judged* in the Greek is *anakrino,* and it means "to scrutinize, examine, and judge." It comes from the word *krino,* which means "to decide judicially." Clearly we see that normal believers, filled with the Spirit of God, are able to judge. Notice also that they are not "rightly judged" by anyone. In other words, people will not understand those who function in this realm of the spirit. It doesn't say they aren't judged. It says they aren't rightly judged. People who judge in the spiritual realm will be criticized and scrutinized. These believers, however, will be justified by the Lord because they are "judging" from His Spirit and heart.

This brings me to the subject we must cover. I can hear someone quoting the oft-referred-to Scripture in Matthew 7:1-5 (NKJV), where Jesus seems to command us not to judge:

> *Judge not, that you be not judged. For with what judgment you judge, you will be judged; and with the measure you use, it will be measured back to you. And why do you look at the speck in your brother's eye, but do not consider the plank in your own eye? Or how can you say to your brother, "Let me remove the speck from your eye"; and look, a plank is in your own eye? Hypocrite! First remove the plank from your own eye, and then you will see clearly to remove the speck from your brother's eye.*

This Scripture is almost always cited as a declaration not to judge. We are told that judging is wrong. We are told that if we judge, we will be judged! However, if we investigate this Scripture more closely, we find that is not what is being said. We are being told that if there are areas of our lives that are not in line with God and His Word, we should refrain from judging. The admonition, however, is to get things right and correct so we can judge righteously. The need for righteous judgment is critical. Without righteous judgment there is NO JUSTICE. When there is NO

JUSTICE, culture and society go off the rails. Ecclesiastes 8:11 (NKJV) shows the lack of justice produces a chaotic state in society:

> *Because the sentence against an evil work is not executed speedily, therefore the heart of the sons of men is fully set in them to do evil.*

When no justice is served effectively, it eliminates a sense of fear, which typically holds people in check. The result is a society out of order and devouring itself.

I was in Singapore and was being hosted by a retired judge from the High Court, which is one step below the Supreme Court of the land. He was explaining to me the reason for the low crime rate in their society. They are a democratic society just like the United States is. However, he explained that instead of making the individual's right the ultimate goal, society as a whole was esteemed.

In other words, the litmus test of their judicial system was not so much how things affected individuals as much as how they affected the society and culture as a whole. The result has been very little crime, less poverty, and a peaceful place within which to live and function. They do not deal with the sense of entitlement that plagues us Americans. The people of the culture have bred into them a sense of honor, wholesome fear, and a desire to be a productive part of culture. I am not saying that Singapore is "better" than America. I am saying, however, that when we exalt the individual above the whole, there will be a breakdown in society. Judgment that produces justice for all must involve valuing society above individual rights and privileges. This has to be taken into account in judicial activities. Decisions cannot be made just on the basis of what is good for one. They have to be made on the basis of what is good for the community and culture of which the one is a member.

When Jesus said don't judge lest you be judged, He was not saying we shouldn't judge. He was declaring that we shouldn't judge if things are not correct in our own lives. If we judge without things spiritually lined up in our lives, then we open ourselves to judgment. The truth is, if we step into a place of judgment without having been judged ourselves, we WILL be judged. The result can be devastating to us.

The devil from his legal position as our adversary—*antidikos* in the Greek—will present a case against us before the Courts of Heaven. We can then find ourselves embroiled in legal issues in the spirit. This is because we have "judged" without first being "judged" or getting things set in order.

Notice in the Scripture that Jesus said if we take the time and effort to get the beam or log out of our eye, *"we will see"* how to get the speck out of another's eye. In other words, we will be able to judge with righteous judgment and help one another. The admonition here isn't to not judge. The admonition is to judge ourselves first so we can then judge rightly. This is what the apostle Paul says in 1 Corinthians 11:31-32 (NKJV).

> *For if we would judge ourselves, we would not be judged. But when we are judged, we are chastened by the Lord, that we may not be condemned with the world.*

When we allow judgment into our lives through the Holy Spirit, we then become those who can render judgment. Paul further said that God judges or chastens us so we won't be condemned with the world. We will escape the consequences of sin, which the world will face. God's chastening and judging hand is actually His mercy at work. It does these two things: It causes us to escape any and all condemnation which the world will suffer, and also sets us into place so we can render judgment without the fear of being judged! This is absolutely necessary if we are to see justice enacted on earth.

Again, we need natural judges but also spiritual ones so God's passion and heart can be seen in the world. The question is, will we allow the work of God to be done in us so we can take our place as "judges" in the realm of the spirit? God needs us to be positioned as judges in the Courts of Heaven. Through prayers, decrees, and declarations, we will be able to see things shift in the spirit realm so they change and line up with God's passion in the natural realm.

I would like to share three things that happened to me in regard to this concept of being a "judge" in the spirit. The first one occurred several years ago now. Mary and I were away on vacation in Hawaii. I had a very vivid dream that shook me. In my dream, an angelic being appeared to me. There was a "seat" hanging in the atmosphere that I knew I could sit in. (Sitting in a seat quite often refers to sitting in a governmental/judicial place, such as a throne.) I took my place in this seat. The angel then handed me a check. Instead of it being a check for money, on it was written a requirement. I understood that something was being required of me to sit in this seat. Since it was in the form of a check, God was saying, "I am giving you the grace you need to fulfill the requirement to sit in this seat." On the check was written, "No more alcohol." I know there will be those who will condemn me because I at that time drank some wine and enjoyed it.

I saw nothing wrong with this and, quite honestly, still do not. I have no problem with those believers who, in moderation, partake of alcoholic beverages. This is just my personal opinion. I respect others' views, but this is mine.

I knew, however, that God was saying to me, "In the place I want you to function from, you cannot partake of alcohol." Later, I would become aware that God was asking me to walk as a Nazarite in the spirit world. The Nazarite vow is found in Numbers 6:1-8 (NKJV) and includes three requirements. They were not allowed to drink wine, touch anything dead, nor cut their hair:

> *Then the Lord spoke to Moses, saying, "Speak to the children of Israel, and say to them: 'When either a man or woman consecrates an offering to take the vow of a Nazirite, to separate himself to the Lord, he shall separate himself from wine and similar drink; he shall drink neither vinegar made from wine nor vinegar made from similar drink; neither shall he drink any grape juice, nor eat fresh grapes or raisins. All the days of his separation he shall eat nothing that is produced by the grapevine, from seed to skin. All the days of the vow of his separation no razor shall come upon his head; until the days are fulfilled for which he separated himself to the Lord, he shall be holy. Then he shall let the locks of the hair of his head grow. All the days that he separates himself to the Lord he shall not go near a dead body. He shall not make himself unclean even for his father or his mother, for his brother or his sister, when they die, because his separation to God is on his head. All the days of his separation he shall be holy to the Lord.'"*

These three things have ramifications for us in the New Testament as we consecrate our lives to the Lord. To not drink wine speaks of being under the influence of nothing but the Holy Spirit. We are to be sober and filled with the Holy Spirit and His power. This is why the apostle Paul wrote in Ephesians 5:18-21 (NKJV) that we were to be filled with the Spirit:

> *And do not be drunk with wine, in which is dissipation; but be filled with the Spirit, speaking to one another in psalms and hymns and spiritual songs, singing and making melody in your*

*heart to the Lord, giving thanks always for all things to God the Father in the name of our Lord Jesus Christ, submitting to one another in the fear of God.*

We are to be under no other influence but the Spirit of the living God. When we are, we are empowered to live out the life we are made for. Another requirement of the Nazarite was to not touch a dead person or thing even if it was a close relative. The dead thing would cause defilement, and the consecration would be lost. This speaks of not touching "dead works." We are not to associate or be part of anything dead. Hebrews 6:1-2 (NKJV) speaks of repenting of dead works:

*Therefore, leaving the discussion of the elementary principles of Christ, let us go on to perfection, not laying again the foundation of repentance from dead works and of faith toward God, of the doctrine of baptisms, of laying on of hands, of resurrection of the dead, and of eternal judgment.*

Dead works is one of the things we are to repent of and move away from. This can be moral and/or ethical issues. I also believe it can speak of dead religious activities that have no life in them. There are definitely dead religious practices that are lifeless and useless in the spirit world. We are to repent of these. Paul spoke of these to Timothy in 2 Timothy 3:5 (NKJV). Paul warns him of people *"having a form of godliness but denying its power. And from such people turn away!"*

Notice that Timothy is exhorted to turn away from these people. Timothy was not to allow into his life those who looked godly but actually had no power to influence him. He wasn't to touch anything that was dead. Traditions, legalisms, and activities void of the life of God were to be avoided. In the New Testament, the vow of the Nazarite isn't about not going to funerals and not being involved with dead corpses. It is about not being influenced by those who have no real spiritual life in them even though they are still naturally breathing. We are not to defile ourselves with dead religion. This would include rituals and traditions with no real spiritual value. They may soothe the conscience but produce no real change or godliness.

The third requirement of a Nazarite was to never cut their hair. My understanding was they could trim their hair to make it manageable but not cut it. This was an outward sign of their inward consecration. Hair speaks of glory and modest covering (1 Corinthians 11:15). Of course, we are familiar with Samson's hair, which represented his strength and anointing and consecration by God. Samson was a Nazarite from his birth, as were Samuel and John the Baptist. All three of them functioned as God's judges on earth. Their Nazarite vow was what allowed them their judgeship in the spirit dimension. It was their consecration by God that granted them their place of authority.

In addition to the "no alcohol" requirement, I also had a dream where my hair was down to my waist. I knew God was telling me that I had a position in the spirit realm as a Nazarite with judge's privileges and responsibilities.

Let me tell you the third and final account. I was in Switzerland teaching on the Courts of Heaven. I was leading the group through an activity of looking into the spirit to see what they were wearing. We all have clothing on in the spirit that speaks of our place, authority, function, and standing there. Remember that the priests in the Old Testament had to wear certain garments and garb to function as a priest. This is seen in Exodus 28:2-4 (NKJV):

> *And you shall make holy garments for Aaron your brother, for glory and for beauty. So you shall speak to all who are gifted artisans, whom I have filled with the spirit of wisdom, that*

*they may make Aaron's garments, to consecrate him, that he may minister to Me as priest. And these are the garments which they shall make: a breastplate, an ephod, a robe, a skill-fully woven tunic, a turban, and a sash. So they shall make holy garments for Aaron your brother and his sons, that he may minister to Me as priest.*

These garments caused Aaron to be recognized in the spiritual realm and granted him a role. As New Testament believers, we, too, are "kings and priests" to our God. We also have garments we have been granted to wear in the spirit realm. These garments give us a place of authority and activity in that dimension. This is why Joshua, a high priest, was given new, fresh garments to wear in Zechariah 3:3-7 (NKJV). It allowed him to function in the realm of the spirit:

*Now Joshua was clothed with filthy garments, and was stand-ing before the Angel. Then He answered and spoke to those who stood before Him, saying, "Take away the filthy garments from him." And to him He said, "See, I have removed your iniquity from you, and I will clothe you with rich robes." And I said, "Let them put a clean turban on his head." So they put a clean turban on his head, and they put the clothes on him. And the Angel of the Lord stood by. Then the Angel of the Lord admonished Joshua, saying, "Thus says the Lord of hosts: 'If you will walk in My ways, and if you will keep My command, then you shall also judge My house, and likewise have charge of My courts; I will give you places to walk among these who stand here.'"*

Notice that when this priest was given fresh, clean clothes to wear, it resulted in him *walking "among these who stand here."* This was in the spirit dimension. His clothes granted him a functional place in a judicial realm of the spirit. The priest had judicial responsibilities. For instance, when someone had leprosy, only the priest could proclaim the person clean so he could return to society. In Leviticus 13:2-3 (NKJV), God makes a decree that priests should examine and make a judgment regarding leprosy:

> *When a man has on the skin of his body a swelling, a scab, or a bright spot, and it becomes on the skin of his body like a leprous sore, then he shall be brought to Aaron the priest or to one of his sons the priests. The priest shall examine the sore on the skin of the body; and if the hair on the sore has turned white, and the sore appears to be deeper than the skin of his body, it is a leprous sore. Then the priest shall examine him, and pronounce him unclean.*

If someone was proclaimed unclean as a result of leprosy, they were ostracized from society. They were not allowed around anyone. They had to proclaim, "Unclean, Unclean," if anyone came near them. It was the priest's job to render this judgment and decision. Also, if someone was cleansed of leprosy, only the priest could verify this change. In Leviticus 14:2 (NKJV), God claims that it is the priest who has the power to proclaim a leper cleansed from his leprosy:

> *This shall be the law of the leper for the day of his cleansing: He shall be brought to the priest.*

The priest had the responsibility of judgment over those with leprosy and in other situations. Being a priest carries responsibility for judgment. For this role in the spirit, we need to put on the right clothes.

Now, back to my encounter in Switzerland. I was not "trying" to see anything concerning myself as I led this group through this activation. I was simply trying to help those to whom I was ministering see themselves in the spirit. Suddenly, I saw myself standing in the spirit realm in black judge's robes. I was somewhat taken back. I didn't yet understand the concept that we could occupy the position of a judge in the spirit dimension. The man who was translating for me, who is very prophetic, then began to laugh. I had not mentioned what I saw. I was still processing it. He suddenly says, "I see an angel here, and every time you say something, he is recording it in writing." I knew this was because of my position as a judge. My words had power and authority in this dimension because of the seat I sat in and what I was wearing in this spirit realm.

Since that time, I have come to realize I have some authority as a judge in the spirit dimension. I try to measure my words because of this authority. I also recognize that I can make decrees because of the position I have been granted. The truth, however, is so can you. Again, the apostle Paul writing to the Corinthian church said those who are spiritual can judge (1 Corinthians 2:15).

There is a place in the Courts of Heaven that we are to operate from. From this place in the Courts of Heaven, we can issue judgments, decrees, and decisions. Heaven needs God's people to take their place as judges in the realms of the spirit. When we occupy these places, our words of decree and declaration can cause things to shift. Things will move in the invisible realm so that which is visible can line up with godly order. We can do this from the Courts of Heaven as those who have been granted the right to judge!

The following is a decree, declaration, and petition you can give to the Lord and His Courts to help you move into this position as a judge.

*I come before You, Lord, who is the Judge of all the earth.*
*As I stand before Your Courts, I request the right to take*
*my place as a judge in Your Courts. I desire, Lord, to*

*be able to release judgments that will set in order Your Kingdom's will on earth. I desire your passion for justice to be seen on the earth. You, Lord, are just in Your nature and person. The justness of who You are is the source of our patience. Your Word declares in Revelation 13:10:*

*He who leads into captivity shall go into captivity; he who kills with the sword must be killed with the sword. Here is the patience and the faith of the saints.*

*I thank You, Lord, for Your justice. I wait for Your justice to be manifested on earth. This is my patience and faith as one who belongs to You. Thank You so much.*

*As I take my place as a judge, I allow the Holy Spirit to "judge" me and chasten me according to Your Word. I invite and yield myself to the searching of the Spirit. I welcome the Holy Spirit's work to reveal and take out of my life any "log" or "beam" that would not allow me to see clearly as a judge. I ask that any wrong perspective, any wrong idea or concept, or any wrong motive be removed from me. I want to give only righteous judgments before You.*

*As a judge in the spirit realm before You, I ask that I might take my seat. The place You have ordained for me to occupy, I by faith take that place. I ask that any mantle and anointing associated with this seat now come upon me. I ask that I might function in the fear of the Lord as a judge in the realm of the spirit. Thanks so much, Lord, for allowing me to make decrees, issue declarations, release prayers, and present petitions before You.*

*I ask, Lord, that things would come to divine order in the natural as things shift in the spirit with these decrees. Lord, may breakthroughs come because of You allowing me to function as a judge from the Courts of Heaven. Thank You so much for this honor and privilege. In Jesus's name, so be it!*

# 10

# PROPHETIC STRATEGIES FOR SPIRITUAL VICTORY

by

## Jennifer LeClaire

After writing many, many books on the practical aspects and theology of spiritual warfare, I decided to write a devotional filled with the Holy Spirit's inspiration for those fighting, along with Scriptures to study, prayers to pray, and decrees and declarations to release over your life. If you engage with the Holy Spirit daily, hear His words, pray these prayers, and follow the wisdom of these Scriptures, you will grow stronger day by day by day.

> Isaiah 43:18-21 (NKJV): *Do not remember the former things, nor consider the things of old. Behold, I will do a new thing, now it shall spring forth; shall you not know it? I will even make a road in the wilderness and rivers in the desert. The beast of the field will honor Me, the jackals and the ostriches, because I give waters in the wilderness and rivers in the desert, to give drink to My people, My chosen. This people I have formed for Myself; they shall **declare My praise.***

## BREAK DEMONIC CYCLES IN YOUR LIFE

### Says God:

You don't have to repeat the same cycles this year that you walked in last year. You can break demonic cycles in your life. You don't have to walk in the same vicious, painful, distressing circles this year. You can interrupt the enemy's plans, but first you have to be aware of the enemy's involvement. You have to see how the wicked one is working to press your buttons, to bring up old memories, to strike at opportune times. You can start this year with a new determination to overcome what has tried over and again to overcome you. I am with you.

### Read:

2 Corinthians 10:3-6; Matthew 4:17; John 8:32

### Prayer:

*Father, help me discern the destructive demonic cycles that manifest in my life. And give me the strategy to overcome every wicked plot against my life.*

### Decree:

*I decree the enemy's plans in my life are disrupted, dismantled, and disengaged. I declare demonic cycles are obliterated, in Jesus's name.*

## WINNING THE BATTLE IN THE WILDERNESS

**Says God:**

There will always be a battle in the wilderness—and it's twofold. You'll have to battle your carnal nature that grows impatient in the waiting. You'll be tempted to take matters into your own hands to bring change into your life that only I can bring. You'll grow weary in the waiting if you don't keep your eyes on Jesus. But your enemy will add another dimension of warfare to your wilderness experience, taking advantage of your impatience and weariness to tempt you to give up altogether. Your promised land is ahead. Join Me in the war against your flesh and against the enemy of your soul.

**Read:**

Matthew 4:1-11; Hebrews 6:12; Galatians 6:9

**Prayer:**

*Father, I will walk through any wilderness You lead me into, but please keep me from temptation. Help me to walk and not grow weary.*

**Decree:**

*I decree I am strong in the Lord and in the power of His might. I declare I am able to walk through any wilderness through His grace and by His mercy, in Jesus's name.*

## Your Enemy Is Not Impenetrable

**Says God:**

Goliath had a helmet of bronze, a coat of mail, and a bronze spear between his shoulders. This giant—this enemy—seemed impenetrable. But I tell you, your enemy's armor is not impenetrable. Your enemy is no match for the sword of the Spirit. Your enemy actually has no armor. Your enemy is vulnerable to the Word of God coming out of your mouth. But your mind is penetrable in the unrenewed areas. Your mind is the point of entry where your enemies make you think and even believe that their armor is impenetrable. David knew his God, ran to the battle line, and saw victory. You can too.

**Read:**

1 Samuel 17:48-49; 1 Chronicles 29:10-13; Isaiah 26:3

**Prayer:**

*Thank You, Lord, that You have given me stronger armor than any Goliath could hope for. Help me see myself as I am in Christ. Help me see the victory beyond the enemy's intimidation.*

**Decree:**

*I decree and declare every Goliath in my life shall fall flat on his face. I decree victory over every giant overshadowing God's blessings in my life, in Jesus's name.*

## SUBMITTING TO ME MEANS RESISTING THE ENEMY

### Says God:

When you don't resist the devil's plans, plots, and ploys against your life, you are not submitting yourself to Me. I have given you strong and sage advice and instruction in My Word. I have told you plainly to submit yourself to My Spirit, resist enemy spirits and they will flee from you. When you don't resist fear, when you don't cast down vain imaginations, when you don't resist demon powers in their various workings against your life, you are resisting My wisdom. So, resist the enemy at his onset. Don't wait until oppression washes over you. I will always deliver you from the enemy's hand when you obey My Word. Resist.

### Read:

James 4:7; 1 Peter 5:9; Matthew 16:23

### Prayer:

*Lord, thank You for this revelation that submitting
to You and resisting the devil work hand in hand.
Give me the strength to resist with everything
in me and not cave into the pressure.*

### Decree:

*I decree I have the power and might of God within me
to resist every enemy attack. I declare that oppression
is broken off my mind and body, in Jesus's name!*

## BELIEVE MY PROMISES OF PROVISION

**Says God:**

Blessed are the poor in spirit, but I have not called you to walk with less than enough. I am the God of more than enough. I have more than enough provision, and I want to pour it out upon you liberally. Your part is to believe My great and precious promises of provision over your life. Your part is to fight the good fight of faith over your finances. Your part is to bind the hand of the thief who comes to steal, kill, and destroy. Your part is to keep your mouth in line with My Word and stop talking about what you don't have. Your part is to put your hand to the plow and give Me something to bless. Don't be deceived. I am your Provider.

**Read:**

2 Corinthians 9:8; Job 38:41; Luke 12:7

**Prayer:**

*Father, I believe. Help my unbelief when the enemy is filling my head with thoughts of lack. I bind the voice and the hand of the enemy over my finances!*

**Decree:**

*I decree my God has more than enough resources to provide all my needs. I declare that all my needs are met—and then some, in Jesus's name!*

## I Need Your Undivided Attention

**Says God:**

I long to sit with you—to hide you under the shadow of My wings day and night. If you will just give me a few minutes, I can change your life. I can change your perspective. I can change your thoughts. I can teach you things. I can show you things. But I need your undivided attention. I've authorized mercy for you. I've authorized prayer answers for you. The enemy wants to steal away the answers and delay the answers. I see the distractions and the enemy interference. It's like static on a radio that makes it difficult to hear the message. Sit with Me and My voice will rise above the static, and you will hear the answers the enemy has been working to keep from you.

**Read:**

Proverbs 2:2-5; Isaiah 26:3; Lamentations 3:25

**Prayer:**

*Father, I give You my time and I give You my heart. Help me to overcome the distractions that work like little foxes to spoil my vine and my time with You.*

**Decree:**

*I decree that the enemy's static is silenced, and God's transmissions reach my heart. I declare that God is answering my prayers and delay is broken over my life, in Jesus's name.*

## DEPLOY MY JOY AS A WEAPON

### Says God:

My joy is your strength. My joy is a strong weapon. Deploy My joy against the discouragement that attacks your soul. Deploy My joy unspeakable and full of glory against the darkness that tries to overtake you. Deploy My joy against the depression that wants to sideline you from your destiny. My joy is within you. Let the river of joy flow from within you and overwhelm the enemies that want to bring you down and take you out.

### Read:

Romans 15:13; Philippians 4:4; Proverbs 17:22

### Prayer:

*Father, thank You for your joy unspeakable and full of glory. Help me to deploy your joy in the face of every enemy attack so I can stand strong and sing Your song.*

### Decree:

*I decree the joy I express in the Lord will overwhelm the enemy's plans and send confusion into his camp. I decree I am wading through the river of the joy of the Lord, in Jesus's name.*

## WHEN THE ENEMY IS BREATHING DOWN YOUR NECK

**Says God:**

When you feel the enemy breathing down your neck, keep running the race. Demons work to intimidate you, to harass you, and to deceive you. Their hot breath on your neck can make it seem like they could strike you down at any moment. In that moment refuse to focus on the enemy behind you and intentionally focus on the God inside you. Draw near to Me, and I will draw near to you. Then you will feel the sweet peace of My Spirit and a fresh wind of My anointing that overshadows the enemy's hot breath on your neck.

**Read:**

Hebrews 12:1-3; Exodus 33:14; Acts 2:1-4

**Prayer:**

*Father, the enemy's breath seems to have a voice.*
*Help me to embrace the wind of Your Spirit when*
*the enemy is huffing and puffing at my back.*

**Decree:**

*I decree that I outpace every enemy force, like Elijah*
*outpaced Ahab after the showdown at Mount*
*Carmel. I declare the wind of Your Spirit is at*
*my back, empowering me, in Jesus's name.*

## Tap into the Anointing to War

**Says God:**

Jesus was anointed and went about doing good and healing all who were oppressed of the devil. He had an anointing to heal, but He also had an anointing to war. He used that anointing for war to do good, not evil. Many times, you will encounter people who are doing you wrong, who are visiting you with evil intentions. Use your warfare anointing to return good for evil and you will be like Jesus, your Savior. Return good for evil and trust Me to bring vindication. I am the warrior, but I don't fight like the world fights. Neither should you.

**Read:**

Acts 10:38; Exodus 15:3; Isaiah 42:13

**Prayer:**

*Father, help me remember the anointing for war is not meant to be aimed toward people but demon powers. Teach me to war like You war and to love like You love.*

**Decree:**

*I decree Christ's anointing operating in my life destroys the works of darkness at every turn. I declare I fight like my heavenly Father fights, in Jesus's name.*

## DISCERN THE VOICE SPEAKING TO YOU

**Says God:**

Paul the apostle explained there are many voices in the spirit. John the apostle later warned you not to believe every spirit, but to test them. There are many spirits in the world, and they all have something to say. They all have an assignment. Vain imaginations are a vehicle for that assignment. Jesus warned to be careful how you listen. Listen closely to the thoughts that enter your mind. They are not all My thoughts, and they are not all your thoughts. The enemy's voice travels in the form of a thought. Judge your thoughts, test the spirits, discern the voice. This is a key to winning the battle in your mind.

**Read:**

1 Corinthians 14:10; 1 John 4:1; Mark 4:24

**Prayer:**

*Father, help me not to be deceived by voices that mimic Yours, twist truth into lies, and try to lead me astray. Help me to discern the many voices in the spirit.*

**Decree:**

*I decree every counterfeit voice working to infiltrate my soul is shut out and shut up. I declare I hear the voice of the Holy Spirit and cast down every other whisper, in Jesus's name.*

## EMBRACE THE SPIRIT OF COOPERATION

### Says God:

Don't fight and war with your brothers and sisters over titles and promotions and other blessings. Where there is unity, I will command a blessing that you cannot contain. I will command a blessing that forces you to cooperate with another to reap that harvest because there is more than enough for all My children. Dare to believe Me today and to stretch yourself further than you did yesterday. Understand and know you can overcome whatever is facing you down when you work with your spiritual family. You will overcome together.

### Read:

Psalm 133; Nehemiah 4:6; Ephesians 4:3

### Prayer:

*Father, help me to honor my brothers and sisters in Christ. Help me to help them do what they are called to do and avoid all striving, for Your glory.*

### Decree:

*I decree strife cannot make its way into my relationships. I declare I am one with my brothers and sisters in the Lord, and we will accomplish great things together, in Jesus's name.*

## Loose Yourself from the Spirit of Infirmity

### Says God:

The spirit of infirmity is sneaky. It will come to attack from time to time, bringing sickness and disease and strange ailments for which the doctors can't find solid diagnoses and can't seem to cure. But I am the God who heals you and removes sickness from you. I am the One who paid the price for your complete healing so you can walk in divine health. I am the One who has the power to drive the spirit of infirmity away from you as you command it to loose you, in Jesus's name.

### Read:

Exodus 23:25; Psalm 91:10; Psalm 103:3

### Prayer:

*Father, thank You for Your healing power that works in me. Thank You for providing a way of escape from the spirit of infirmity by Your blood.*

### Decree:

*I decree the spirit of infirmity must flee from me now! I declare sickness and disease dies when it comes in contact with my body, for His glory, in Jesus's name.*

## WAGE WAR WITH THE PROPHETIC WORD

**Says God:**

When you look back at the prophetic words I have released over your life, you'll know better how to fight what is attacking you in the next season. The words I speak to you are spirit and life. Fight the enemy's resistance with those words. Those prophecies that came from My heart over your life will invigorate you in the battle. They will arm you for war against the specific assignment the enemy has launched against you. They will strengthen your arms to lift up your shield of faith. They are revelation for you to war with. Look back at the prophetic words, and the season you are in will make more sense.

**Read:**

1 Timothy 1:18; 2 Chronicles 20:20

**Prayer:**

*Father, remind me of the prophetic words I've long ago forgotten about. Arm me with the revelation of Your will for my life so I can stand in faith without wavering.*

**Decree:**

*I decree every prophetic word spoken over my life shall come to pass, despite enemy resistance. I declare God's words over me shall not return void, in Jesus's name.*

## DETERMINE TO FIGHT THE GOOD FIGHT

**Says God:**

I've called you to be an agent of change in the earth but change never comes without resistance. The enemy will always resist My light, My life, and My love manifesting through you to a dark, hopeless, hateful world. The enemy will resist you directly as you work with My Spirit to bring the truth to the people I love. But rest assured in this: as you determine to fight the good fight of faith, the resistance will make you stronger. So, get determined, resist the resistance. I will strengthen you to fight if you determine you're willing.

**Read:**

1 Timothy 6:12; James 4:7; Matthew 5:16

**Prayer:**

*Father, help me resist the resistance. Strengthen me in my inner man to stand and withstand in the evil day. I am willing to stand against the wiles of the enemy.*

**Decree:**

*I decree every resistance to God's good, perfect, and acceptable will must bow to Jesus. I declare I am a change agent on earth, empowered by the Holy Spirit, in Jesus's name.*

## BEWARE OF SPIRITUAL WARFARE DITCHES

**Says God:**

It so grieves Me how some of My children refuse to believe in the existence of the evil one when My Word of truth points to his work over and over again. But it also grieves me when my children fail to see the victory Christ won for them when He shamed principalities and powers through the work of the cross. There are two great deceptions on earth My beloved ones fall into. They ignore the enemy, or they cower to his fearful agendas. Don't let that be you. Understand the reality of your enemy but understand I have given you victory over every spiritual foe in the name of Jesus. Remember that when his attack rages against you and strengthen your brothers and sisters.

**Read:**

1 Peter 5:8; Colossians 2:15; 2 Corinthians 2:11

**Prayer:**

*Father, please warn me if I am in danger of falling into one of these ditches. Help me focus on the victory I have over the enemy, but never underestimating my foes.*

**Decree:**

*I decree the enemy is trapped in his own deceptive ditch of lies. I declare my victory over the powers of darkness and subtle deceptions that try to find a way into my soul, in Jesus's name.*

## Receive a War Strategy That Shocks the Enemy

**Says God:**

Just as Father was with Jesus, He is with you. And your Father in Heaven is a master strategist. No enemy attack takes Him by surprise. No whispered lie the wicked one releases convinces Him to leave you. Yes, the devil is the accuser, and he accuses you to Father. He accuses Father to you. He accuses you to yourself, and he causes you to look for someone to blame for your warfare. Don't fall into this demonic trap. Turn to your Father in Heaven for a strategy of war that will surprise the enemy of your soul. You cannot lose.

**Read:**

John 17:20; Revelation 12:10; Hebrews 13:5

**Prayer:**

*Father, thank You for standing with me in battle. Help me avoid the temptation to point fingers at You or anybody else when I am under attack. Give me a strategy to overcome.*

**Decree:**

*I decree the accuser of the brethren is cast down from my heart and mind. I declare my battle plan will shock the enemy and cause him to flee, in Jesus's name.*

## PUT ON CHRIST

**Says God:**

It's good that you have put on your whole armor, but you also need to put on Christ. Walk in Him. Walk in a revelation of who He is in you and who you are in Him. When you put on Christ and determine in your heart to align your character with His, you will maintain an authority over the wicked one. When you put on Christ and walk in Him, low-level devils that derailed you in past seasons will not attempt to harass you. And when the higher-ranking spirits launch fiery darts against you, you will laugh at your enemies just like your Father in Heaven because you know nothing shall by any means harm you.

**Read:**

Galatians 3:27; 2 Peter 3:18; Romans 8:5

**Prayer:**

*Father, thank You for equipping me with spiritual armor to fight my battles. Help me not neglect to get dressed for war against armed and dangerous spirits.*

**Decree:**

*I decree my armor—the armor God Himself gave me—hinders hindering spirits targeting me. I declare I have put on Christ and I walk in Him every day and at all times, in Jesus's name.*

## LOVE CAN WORK AS A WEAPON

### Says God:

Use love as an advantage over your adversary. Love can work as a weapon for you in the spiritual battle. For although you are ultimately wrestling demons in the spirit world, the enemy often works through people to harm you with lies, accusations, and other harmful words. Walk in love. Overcome evil with good. Buy a gift for the one the enemy has stirred against you or offer a sincere compliment. In doing so, you will heap coals of Holy Spirit's conviction on their head, and you can both walk in freedom.

### Read:

Galatians 5:22-23; Romans 12:20; Romans 12:21

### Prayer:

*Father, remind me when my anger rises against a person the enemy is using against me that they don't realize what they are really doing. Help me walk in love.*

### Decree:

*I decree my love walk is on fire and burns up every agenda of the enemy to turn me into a vengeful person. I declare I walk in love even with those who hate me, in Jesus's name.*

## EXAMINE YOUR THOUGHTS

### Says God:

Examine your thoughts. Are you thinking like Me or are you thinking like your adversary, who roams about like a roaring lion seeking someone to devour? Are you thinking My thoughts, or are you meditating on the thoughts of fear, doubt, and unbelief the enemy is injecting into your soul? Are you aware of your thought life with all its machinations? As a man thinks in his heart, so is he. My thoughts are higher than your thoughts, but the enemy's thoughts you take as your own will bring you low. Stop and think about what you are thinking about. The battle is in the mind, but the war is for your heart.

### Read:

Isaiah 55:8-9; Joshua 1:8; Proverbs 23:7

### Prayer:

*Father, help me to think about what I am thinking about. Help me recognize the enemy's intrusion into my thought life immediately and reject his poisonous lies.*

### Decree:

*I decree the enemy's thoughts are locked out of the sanctuary of my mind. I declare the meditations of my heart are pleasing in God's sight and torment the enemy, in Jesus's name.*

# The Enemy Is the Same Yesterday, Today, and Forever

## Says God:

I am your God. I am the same yesterday, today, and forever. The enemy of your soul is competing for godship in your life. He is also the same yesterday, today, and forever. Satan has no new tricks. He has no new strategies. He has no new tactics. He doesn't need any because mankind continues to fall for the tried-and-true lies. Rise up above your contemporaries who are so easily deceived by the lust of the flesh, the lust of the eyes, and the pride of life, and choose to serve Me with your whole heart. Stay close to Me and you will not fall for the devil's lies.

## Read:

Hebrews 13:8; John 8:44; Revelation 12:9

## Prayer:

*Father, help me discern the truth from a lie. Your Word is truth. Put me in remembrance of Your Word when the enemy is working to deceive me with crafty lies.*

## Decree:

*I decree every enemy strategy and tactic is null and void in my life. I declare I discern every lie of the wicked one and reject it with everything in me, in Jesus's name.*

## JESUS IS THE STRONGER MAN

**Says God:**

Jesus rightly described your enemy as a strongman. But Jesus is the stronger Man. Jesus is greater than any enemy stronghold and can deliver you from evil. Cry out to Me in His name and you will meet face to face with your deliverer. Jesus will empower you to overcome the strongman who has kept you in bondage. By way of the resurrection life and power that dwells inside you, He will empower you to break free from every tie that binds you to death. The strongman may have you bound, but the stronger Man in you will lead you into liberty.

**Read:**

Matthew 12:29; John 10:10; Psalm 107:6

**Prayer:**

*Father, thank You for delivering me from evil. Thank You for empowering me to overcome every strongman that works to kill, steal, and destroy my life.*

**Decree:**

*I decree every strongman holding my life hostage is discovered, bound, and cast out. I declare I am spoiling the strongman's house and taking back what he stole, in Jesus's name.*

# I Hear the Chatter Against Your Mind

## Says God:

What worries you doesn't frustrate Me. What keeps you up at night doesn't keep Me up at night. What scares you and steals your peace does not move Me. Do you want to know why? Because I am not giving ear to the voice of the enemy. I hear his chatter against your mind, but it does not move Me. I see your end from your beginning. I created you in My image. I am standing with you, living inside you, and leading and guiding you. Stop allowing the enemy to worry you, keep you up at night, scare you, and steal your peace. Walk with Me.

## Read:

John 16:33; 1 Peter 5:7; Isaiah 9:6

## Prayer:

*Father, help me combat worry that plagues my mind when everything seems to be going wrong all at once. Teach me to walk in peace even when chaos surrounds me.*

## Decree:

*I decree a divine reversal of the demonic chatter against my heart. I declare the voice of worry is silenced and I walk in the peace that passes all understanding, in Jesus's name.*

## ASK ME FOR THE WORD OF WISDOM

### Says God:

I have all wisdom. I have the wisdom you need for every battle you will ever fight. I see the end from the beginning. I'm never blindsided by what blindsides you. Ask Me for a word of wisdom about the enemies plotting and planning against you. Have I not promised to show you things to come? Ask Me for a word of wisdom about the enemy's schemes against your church. Let Me use you to warn, sound the trumpet, and blow the alarm. Use this spiritual gift as a tactic in war.

### Read:

1 Corinthians 12:8; Proverbs 4:6-7; James 1:5

### Prayer:

*Father, I am asking for wisdom for the warfare I am facing now and the warfare that will come against me in the future. Give me a heads-up. Show me what the enemy is doing and how to overcome before the battle begins raging.*

### Decree:

*I decree the wisdom of God I receive confounds the enemy of my soul in every battle. I declare the spiritual gifts inform my spiritual warfare and I am victorious, in Jesus's name.*

## BE CAREFUL WHO YOU GO TO BATTLE WITH

### Says God:

When you go into battle, choose your fellow soldiers wisely. Do not take the foolish. Do not take the fearful. Do not take the presumptuous. Do not take those who are unskilled in battle. There is a time of training and a time of war. If you take people into war with you who are not properly prepared or who do not trust Me with their lives, you will open a door to the enemy in your camp and people will get hurt. You will have to expend your energy rescuing them from the snare of the fowler. You will bring more warfare on yourself. Be careful who you go to battle with.

### Read:

Judges 7; Luke 14:31; Deuteronomy 24:5

### Prayer:

*Father, give me wisdom to choose who I trust to war with me and send me people who are trustworthy to take into battle. Help me discern who really has my back.*

### Decree:

*I decree demonic agendas are met with divine deployments on my behalf. I declare I am warring unto victory with few skilled warriors just like Gideon did, in Jesus's name.*

## STOP FIGHTING EVERY BATTLE ALONE

### Says God:

Two are better than one. One can put a thousand to flight. Two can put ten thousand to flight. Yes, there are some battles you will have to fight alone. There are some enemies you will have to gain victory over in your own right by My authority and grace. But I have not called you to fight every battle alone. I have called you to go two by two into the enemy's camp like the lepers who sat at the gate. I have called you to be part of an army who goes in to battle the strongman and take the spoils. Stop fighting alone. Ask your brothers and sisters for the help you need to overtake the devil's plans for your life.

### Read:

Deuteronomy 32:30; Joshua 23:10; Leviticus 26:8

### Prayer:

*Father, help me discern when I need reinforcements in the fight. Give me the grace of humility to understand I need help and the willingness to ask for the help I need, in Jesus's name.*

### Decree:

*I decree a synergy in the spirit for warfare against the strongman. I declare victory behind my wildest imagination is my portion in battle, in Jesus's name.*

## DON'T OVERREACT TO THE ENEMY'S MANEUVERS

**Says God:**

Be careful not to overreact to the enemy's maneuvers. He's watching. He's examining you from top the bottom. He's exploring your reactions to his fiery darts. Will you rise up with the shield of faith and quench his onslaught? Or will you speak words of fear to your friends and family? Will you become anxious and overwhelmed? Or will you become bold as a lion in the face of the enemy's persecution against your life? Don't overreact. Stay calm. I am your peace. Look to Me, and I will help you stay the course to victory.

**Read:**

2 Corinthians 12:9; Proverbs 28; Colossians 3:15

**Prayer:**

*Father, help me stay alert in the spirit so that
I quickly recognize the enemy's presence. Put a
guard over my mouth and draw me close to You
when the enemy is raging against me.*

**Decree:**

*I decree a deluge of anxiety, pressure, and persecution against
the enemy. I declare I walk in the Spirit and respond in
the Spirit to every enemy onslaught, in Jesus's name.*

## WALK AS CHRIST WALKED THE EARTH

**Says God:**

Selfishness opens the door to the devourer. Selflessness paves the way for Me to move. When you act selfishly, you make poor decisions based on your needs and your needs alone. You end up in dangerous positions where the enemy can strike you because whatever is not of faith is sin. Selfishness is not of faith. When you walk in selflessness, you are walking as Christ walked on earth. The enemy had no place in Him. He did not consider His own body or His own desires, but the desire of His heavenly Father who sent Him. Crucify self and slam the door on the enemy.

**Read:**

Philippians 2:3-4; Proverbs 19:17; Galatians 5:24

**Prayer:**

*Father, help me to crucify my flesh. Give me the strength to pick up my cross and follow Jesus. Show me the bigger picture in the battle so I can get my mind off myself and on to others.*

**Decree:**

*I decree the devourer of my flesh is disallowed and disavowed. I declare temptations of the flesh are overcome by the force of my will to follow Jesus and I will overcome, in Jesus's name.*

## Beware the Lies in Your Eyes

**Says God:**

Your spiritual enemies and your foes are trying to bind you and blind you. Your wicked opponents are trying to throw lies in your eyes so you cannot discern the life I have for you. It's time to turn the tables. It's time to bind the enemy according to the authority Father has given to you in the name of Jesus. It's time to blind the foes with the light of the Word. It's time to speak life and allow My Spirit to battle with and for you. Christ's words are spirit and life. Speak the Word of truth, light, and life and you will see clearly to bind your enemy and take back what he stole while you could not see him.

**Read:**

Ephesians 5:8; John 1:5; Matthew 16:19

**Prayer:**

*Father, open the eyes of my heart and help me see what I cannot see. Break off the blinders the enemy has erected around my vision so I can discern the lies rightly.*

**Decree:**

*I decree every demonic entity attacking my vision is bound. I declare my spiritual eyesight is clear, and I discern and resist the darkness that is working to overtake me, in Jesus's name.*

## DON'T BOW TO ANY OTHER SPIRIT BUT MINE

**Says God:**

Don't bow down to the ways of the world. Don't bow down to the imaginations of your heart. Continue to bow down to Me. Bow a knee to Me. Don't bow to the spirit of fear. Don't bow to that spirit of discouragement. I know it's tempting to give up and quit and run in the other direction. But don't do it! Run to Me. Run to the throne. Come boldly to My throne. My throne is a throne of grace. It's a throne of mercy. It's a throne where you can come at any moment, knowing that I will receive you, because you are in Christ.

**Read:**

Philippians 2:9–11; Psalm 95:6; Psalm 5:7

**Prayer:**

*Father, I bow down to You and You alone. You reign supreme in my life. Help me run to You and not away from You when the pressure from the spirit world feels overwhelming.*

**Decree:**

*I decree fear, discouragement, and imaginations bow to the Christ in me. I declare my heart bows to the Lord Jesus and to Him alone, in Jesus's name.*

# 11

# A GODLY DEFIANCE

by

*Jon and Jolene Hamill*

This chapter tells you specifically how to partner with God to receive His turnaround, align with His turnaround, and decree His turnaround to impact your world. You probably would not be exploring these pages unless you were seeking a change in your trajectory from the Lord yourself!

Maybe you are seeking a turnaround for your loved ones, for your marriage, your health, your business, or for a deeper relationship with Jesus. Many of the strongest breakthroughs are intensely personal, and we share them with the goal of equipping you to overcome challenges in your own life and family. Turnaround time!

Above all, you will learn to make decrees from your position of kingship before God's throne, seated with Christ in heavenly places and ruling with Him to impact your world. The nations will understand this clearly in the days ahead. You and I are now being granted a rare opportunity to both gain understanding and pioneer a new movement.

We are in an hour similar to the era of the American Revolution, except this time the authoritarian regime contending to steal our freedom is actually embedded within our own government and culture. In this way, we have perhaps most closely resembled pre-World War II Nazi Germany.

Too extreme? Keep in mind Germany was a strong Christian nation, actually the birthplace of the Protestant Reformation, when it was taken over. Propaganda developed by the Nazis radically shifted their nation and culture away from their covenantal foundations, and toward dictatorship. More, the propaganda infused within many, youth especially, a welcoming of governance by dictatorship.

Keep this in mind: All totalitarian movements seek to indoctrinate coming generations. They target our children. This is happening in the United States at a dramatically accelerated rate. And it puts in jeopardy those you love the most.

The good news is that the Lord is giving us a way not only to stem the tide but reverse it. It is against this backdrop that, in 2021, the Lord encountered me and again decreed a season of turnaround. As you will discover, this turnaround is on a personal level first, then to our nation and nations. We believe it will become the most comprehensive turnaround in modern history. For His glory!

All this noted, our hour of history mandates godly defiance to forces seeking to define our future apart from God's desire. As Ben Franklin famously observed, "Rebellion to tyrants is obedience to God."

I am reminded of the courageous rabbi and his wife who lit a Hanukkah menorah in their window overlooking an oversized Nazi flag. Daniella Greenbaum wrote a powerful recounting for the *New York Times:* "In 1932, just before Hitler's rise to power, their menorah shone brightly for all their neighbors to see. Its light—and the meaning behind it—was made all the more incandescent given the symbol of Jew-hatred hanging from the building across the street."[1]

According to the article, on the back of their Hanukkah a simple declaration was inscribed, borne of this act of godly defiance. Rachel Posner, the wife of renowned German rabbi Avika Posner wrote: "'Death to Judah' so the flag says. 'Judah will live forever,' so the light answers.'"

Friend, what is your own light speaking? As we embark on this journey through God's turnaround decrees, please know that your burning lamp is the ultimate decree. One small candle can still light a thousand. It overcomes all the encroaching darkness, if only you resolve to shine.


## I WILL SAVE YOUR CHILDREN!

*"...I will contend with the one who contends with you, and I will save your children"* (Isaiah 49:25 CSB).

It was the sound every parent dreads. When our daughter, Ashley, was around four years old, she slipped on the stairs and fell to the bottom of the basement. Seemingly endless thumps accompanied piercing screams. I (Jon) raced down the stairs after her, praying like a madman. It was a complete surprise to find my daughter relatively calm at the foot of the stairs, seemingly barely harmed.

All at once, right in the midst of this crisis, "Isaiah 49:25" flashed through my mind. I had no idea what it said. I immediately thought, *Lord, I'm kind of busy here, got my hands full. Could You maybe just recite to me the verse?* But that didn't happen. Instead I rushed my daughter to a local hospital just to make sure she was okay. After a thorough evaluation the doctors could not find even a fracture.

It wasn't until later that night, just before bed, when I finally found time to look up the passage. Keep in mind this incident occurred long before mobile phones or Google could provide instant results with little effort. Instead I did something that might give most of us pause today. I grabbed an actual Bible. With pages. The contents discovered were astonishing given the circumstances.

> "...I will contend with him who contends with you, and I will save your children" (Isaiah 49:25 CSB).

As I prayed, it became clear that this was more than a Scripture over a situation. It was a covenant promise from the Lord. A decree. And the Lord gave this covenantal decree to carry us through the rest of our lives.

*"I will contend...and I will save your children."* From this time forward I knew God was promising to take the initiative in the healing, deliverance, and blessing of my kids. Little did I know how much more I would need this promise from the Lord later in their lives. It soon carried me, and especially my children, through challenges we could then barely even imagine. Rebellion. Discord. Demonic attacks. Damages to heart and soul were all ahead. Yet God remained utterly faithful. And again and again He has brought a turnaround where there seemed to be no way forward!

Let me be clear: Just because the Lord decrees His intervention does not mean you or I have no responsibility in the matter. Instead the opposite is true. The spiritual conflicts Jolene and I had to engage in and overcome were among the highest we have ever experienced. It actually prepared us for the many battles we were going to face nationally.

And honestly, if we had not had the decree promising that the Lord was going to pull our kids through, we would probably have given up long before gaining the victory.

But the other aspect of this is that *both the wars and victories belonged to the Lord, not to us.* We brought love and discipline. But like every parent, sometimes we failed. The promise that the Lord would contend, and save our children, meant that He was the One in charge of the battle. And that His pathway included mending and repairing damage we failed to prevent.

That's really difficult, especially as parents. But we realized that many times the greatest weapon of warfare was simply to let go in the natural and trust Him to fulfill His promise His way.

> For this is what the Lord says, "Even the captives of a mighty man will be taken, and the prey of a tyrant will be delivered; I will contend with the one who contends with you, and I will save your children" (Isaiah 49:25 CSB).

## WHEN GOD INITIATES THE DECREE

I believe Isaiah 49:25 is a decree from the Lord for your life and family. Consider it a sacred gift from the Father that He is initiating in your life just as He did in ours. Claim His promise! Declare His decree. I believe the covenant promise will become a foundation for your turnaround.

It's important to note that the Lord directly initiated this decree in our lives. There are 31,102 verses between the Old Testament and the New Testament. For the Lord to highlight this one, amid a moment of crisis when it was needed the most, shows His incredible watch over all of us.

Here are a few questions: What decrees has the Lord made personal to your life? How? What has He initiated in your life to claim, to declare, to gain? Maybe like me, a specific Scripture was highlighted to you. Maybe you've received a promise within a dream, or a prophetic word from an outside source. These decrees are like a check in the mail to you—signed, sealed, and delivered!

Make a list of them. And then make your decrees!

## RECEIVING AND ACTIVATING YOUR DECREES

Receiving and applying God's turnaround decrees is actually a very simple process. The biggest key is knowing in your heart that the decree actually is sourced from God—to you personally, or to your sphere.

In basic terms, the word of the Lord is His decree over you. You must declare it to activate it. Call those things that are not as though they are! As David observed in Psalm 2:7 (CSB), *"I will declare the Lord's decree."*

I'll never forget rediscovering Christmas after I was born again. The same carols from my childhood came alive with fresh meaning and life. I was hungry to learn, especially how to hear the voice of God for myself. And God answered with a precious gift.

I heard His voice with clarity. This is what He said to me: "When you pray in the Name of Jesus, at the leading of the Holy Ghost, you are not just praying, you are prophesying, or calling those things that are not as though they are!"

That's what the decree of the Lord does. It aligns the earth with His directive. Our job is to receive His decree, then declare it. The prophet Isaiah received such a commissioning:

> *And I have put My words in your mouth and have covered you with the shadow of My hand, that I may plant the heavens, lay the foundations of the earth, and say to Zion, "You are My people"* (Isaiah 51:16 NKJV).

## SEVEN STEPS TO RECEIVE AND
## DECLARE GOD'S DECREE

Let's look at seven easy steps to receive and declare God's decree, utilizing Isaiah 49:25 as an example, *"I will save your children!"*

1.  Receive the decree of the Lord. Note that when the Lord gave me His promise to save my children, He spoke a Scripture to claim and declare. What is the Spirit of God conveying to you, either by highlighting the word, by speaking directly by His Spirit, or both? Note the communication of Holy Spirit will never violate the written Scriptures. But He will often give new revelation you have not yet perceived.

2.  Write the decree! So often decrees, dreams, and other communication from Holy Spirit are lost simply because we fail to record what we've received from Him.

3.  Pray in the Spirit. When possible, worship and pray in the Spirit until you sense an unction to declare the decree He has given. Most of the time it will just arise out of your spirit.

4.  Declare the decree! Note the Lord put His word in Isaiah's mouth (see Isaiah 51:16). He did the same with Jeremiah (Jeremiah 1:10-11). By speaking the decree, you are announcing to both the spirit realm and the earthly realm the directive of His governance. Both must yield.

5.  When you decree God's word, the angelic hosts are activated. They must and will respond. Psalm 103:20 (NASB)

shows that the angelic hosts are activated by the voice of His word to perform the directive within the decree: *"Bless the Lord, you His angels, mighty in strength, who perform His word, obeying the voice of His word."* Declare the decree!

6. Train for the turnaround! Adjust your life to gain the fulfillment of what you are seeking. This includes praying, repenting, and turning from any known sin that may give the enemy legal right to block the manifestation.

7. Keep watch over the decree. Many times a decree is not immediately manifested even after it is released. It must be "prayed through." More ahead!

These steps are essential as you partner with the Lord over your children. The promise that God will save is not a magic trump card. No decree is. Sometimes manifestations come instantaneously, other times not. But always you must keep watch in prayer. You must partner with God to birth His decree into manifestation, as He applies it to various cycles and situations of their lives.

And as you partner with the Lord both to receive and declare His decree, praying until its full manifestation, I guarantee it will carry you through many decades if you allow it to. *"I will contend with those who contend with you, and your I children I will save"* (Isaiah 49:25 NIV).

## GOD IS BIGGER THAN UNFORESEEN CHALLENGES

It was the moment every parent dreams of. My daughter, a new graduate from high school, sat us down to ask our perspective on plans she had made for the future. She had decided to pursue a career in the military. "Pray for me, I'm going into the Air Force," she said. Then there was a short pause followed by a flash of a smile. "No, wait. Pray for the Air Force, because I'm going into the Air Force!"

We all laughed around the table. Probably because there might have been at least a little truth in the statement. I knew just what to pray. "Lord, contend with those who contend against my daughter, in the spirit and natural! Deliver her from all harm. Mature her in You. Save our children. AND SAVE THE AIR FORCE!"

Challenges totally arose. But through it all our daughter really did well...eventually. Ashley matured greatly through the process. She mastered new skills in a field that now has become her career. She prospered. During her time of service my daughter met and married a fantastic, highly responsible soldier who loves her wholeheartedly and treats her far better than any guy she ever dated before. They have similar interests. They are secure, stable, and hilarious together. A few years ago they even gave us a beautiful grandchild!

My point? When God promises to contend and save, He goes far beyond what we could ever imagine. This is absolutely true with both of our children.

One recent conversation brought me to tears. It went something like this:

"Dad, do you remember when we were little and you took us to Washington, DC, and we toured the National Mall and all the memorials, and I complained because I thought the mall you were taking us to would actually have stores?"

I cringed. "Uh...yeah, as a matter of fact I do."

"And you know how maybe I judged you for being excessively, overly patriotic ever since?"

My face turned red. I hoped she didn't notice. "Well...yeah."

"Dad, I just want you to know, after being in the Air Force I get it now. I really do. I appreciate like never before the sacrifices made to keep our nation free."

That meant everything to me.

Now let me tell you a secret I've discovered. The same God who is bigger than the unforeseen challenges your children and mine will face is also bigger than the unforeseen challenges we as a nation will face.

The promise remains the same. So does the pathway through to salvation. Even the captives of the mighty will be rescued. Remember, He *"will contend with the one who contends with you. And I will save your children."*

## LESSONS FROM THE JESUS REVOLUTION

The United States right now stands in the balance. Our covenantal inheritance as a nation is far more vulnerable now than most leaders care to admit. We as a nation seem to be in a time similar to the 1960s, an era when new levels of sin and vileness became embraced as a cultural norm. The occult and even satanism went mainstream during the '60s. Sexual sin became celebrated, with protective purity discarded and "free love" embraced as a viable lifestyle. Countless marriages and families were destroyed. Fathers fled. Mothers fled. Children often became the most impacted, infusing despondency, hopelessness, and anger into their hearts. All the while extreme drug use mesmerized the masses and thwarted the true potential of countless individuals.

And a generation who previously considered Judeo-Christian values normative found themselves suddenly at the end of the road.

It was during this tumultuous time when God broke in with a Jesus revolution. A massive tsunami of evangelism swept multitudes into the Kingdom. California coasts especially were filled with baptism services. New wineskins such as Calvary Chapel and the Vineyard movement sprang up. Revelation on spiritual warfare, on apostolic and prophetic ministry, expanded our horizons. Instantaneous healings and deliverances became normative. And Billy Graham filled stadiums as a nation turned to Jesus.

God did it then. Can He do it now? The Lord is looking for forerunners who dare to dream with Him for a dramatic recovery of revival. A new Jesus revolution. It's in our blood. It's part of America's DNA. We are a nation of awakening!

The greater question to ask is, what sparked this Jesus revolution? Preeminently, a massive wave of desperate prayer just beforehand. Fathers and mothers, grandfathers and grandmothers, teachers and leaders fell to their faces and engaged with God over their children. Their intercession forged a Glory pathway for revival to sweep the land.

And it's about to happen again. You can feel it in the atmosphere. A new grace of birthing prayer is being released for the deliverance of this generation. LET MY CHILDREN GO!

## DECREEING AND RECEIVING— THE PROCESS

When God initiates a project, He decrees the end from the beginning:

*I am God, and there is no one like Me, declaring the end and the result from the beginning, and from ancient times the things which have not [yet] been done, saying, "My purpose will be established, and I will do all that pleases Me and fulfills My purpose"* (Isaiah 46:9-10 Amplified Bible).

Many times the manifestation of God's decrees seem almost spontaneous, in real time. Other times the process may seem extended. But in all cases there is a process. Understanding the process helps you to better partner with the Lord through it.

God's decree initiates the process, frames the results, and announces the arrival in its proper timing. But you have to know your partnership is vital to bring it to pass.

In that context it's kind of like having a baby. Especially when contending for the salvation of your children or loved ones to turn to the Lord. No wonder Jesus called it a born-again experience!

First, there's a conception. Then comes hidden growth. On the surface it appears nothing is going on. In reality, every facet of your baby, your answer to prayer, is in development. Then comes the discovery that a miracle is on its way! The beautiful miracle inside is worth living for, even radically changing your lifestyle to prepare the way for.

But it's not easy. No wonder carrying a prayer project has many times been referred to as "carrying a prayer burden."

Now the old-timers had enough sense to pray these burdens through to breakthrough. For some reason many in our generation have let go of this lost art. Decrees alone don't always finish the job. Heed their wisdom and pray through!

That's when there is a birthing. It's time! Often the arrival of God's promise is accompanied by breakthrough declarations. Sometimes it involves intense "birthing prayer" often referred to as travail.

## TRAVAIL AS A WEAPON OF WAR

Recently the Lord really focused Jolene and me on Psalm 6, where "the voice of our tears" is met by God's movement of breakthrough and vindication. One of the key verses He gave us was Isaiah 42:14-15 (CSB): *"...But now, I will groan like a woman in labor* [travail], *gasping breathlessly. I will lay waste mountains...."*

As a guy, I've mostly paid attention to the verse before these two. It's actually how I picture His collaboration with us: *"The Lord advances like a warrior; he stirs up his zeal like a soldier. He shouts, he roars aloud, he prevails over his enemies"* (Isaiah 42:13 CSB). This Scripture verse awakens fire in me every time. I want to join with the Lord to utterly, completely prevail against His enemies, don't you? I want our procession to be so directed by the Lord that He is marching forth in our midst as the conquering King!

And if there's anything I know about the season, it's that the Lord is raising His war cry for battle right now. His zeal is aroused!

But how He wars in this season is very telling. One facet of His warfare is actually compared to *a woman in travail*, bringing to birth His purposes. All that said, travailing prayer is a major weapon of warfare. And it is key to gain His new birth of freedom!

And it is an absolute sign of apostolic fathering and mothering. The greatest apostle in the New Testament described it this way: *"My children, with whom I am again in labor until Christ is formed in you..."* (Galatians 4:19 NASB).

So how do you enter into this dimension of prayer? First and foremost, by praying in the Spirit. When you pray in the Spirit you allow Holy Spirit to intercede through you the precise plans and purposes of the Father. Further, He partners with you to bring to birth His desire: *"Not by might nor by power, but by My Spirit,' says the Lord of hosts"* (Zechariah 4:6 NASB).

> *For we know that the whole creation groans and suffers the pains of childbirth together. ...Now in the same way the Spirit also helps our weakness; for we do not know what to pray for as we should, but the Spirit Himself intercedes for us with groanings too deep for words; and He who searches the hearts knows what the mind of the Spirit is, because He intercedes for the saints according to the will of God* (Romans 8:22, 26-27 NASB).

## BEYOND THE END OF THE ROAD

Alaska, as a breakthrough state, has been highlighted to us in this season. As you can discover in Chapter 6 of our book *Turnaround Decrees*, the Lord mandated Alaska to release a Daniel 7:22 decree that defines the turnaround movement of today, so similar to the Jesus revolution of the 1960s and '70s.

One afternoon we boarded a ferry from the town of Homer. A coastal town on the Kenai peninsula, Homer is known as "the end of the road." There's a very legitimate reason. Homer, Alaska, is the westernmost destination of the entire US highway system. It actually is *the end* of the road!

Maybe you've been there before? Not Homer per se. But maybe your own end of the road?

It happens a lot in the midst of everyday life. It always happens during childbirth! And also when you are bringing to birth the purposes of the Lord. There comes a point when your strongest efforts and noblest intentions still can't get the job done. Your options seem gone, and though you know what God wants, you simply see no way to bring it to pass.

Okay...I see you've got a T-shirt from Homer too.

Opening your heart to God during these situations always secures His assistance. Talk with Him as you would to a friend. Be honest with Him. You'll soon find something deep within you summoning you to arise. To pray. To decree. To take the right steps and advance His way. In process—this is a word from the Lord to you—*the end of the road will become a gateway to your new beginnings.* And you'll leave behind a trail of broken-down barriers which once defined your limitations. Decree this now!

Fair warning here for those who aspire to become forerunners. You will always want to know what's beyond the end of the road. Which is why, in Homer, we boarded a boat with the Alaskan wilderness as our destination.

Besides our team there were maybe 20 passengers at best when the ferry left the dock, which made conversations easy to hear. Someone on the other side of the boat started talking about Jesus, and it caught my attention. To my utter surprise I found myself speaking with an older apostolic evangelist who had traveled eight million miles around the world ministering the Gospel.

And in the late 1960s, he unexpectedly became a father of the Jesus revolution.

Now what are the chances, leaving "the end of the road" on a ferry with 20 passengers to an island wilderness in Alaska, that a father of the Jesus Movement would also be on board? My spirit stood at attention, for all the right reasons.

Dale Van Steenis told us the story of how he witnessed the spark of the Jesus Movement firsthand. He was coaching a pastor in Southern California who had given up all hope after his church split for the third time. While with them he attended a weekly prayer meeting at the church, which the pastor had facilitated for almost a decade. At one time the prayer meeting was packed. But now only a few die-hards showed up.

Die-hards mostly anyway. Of course the discreet prayers of the pastor would have revealed he was actually seeking the Lord to move on. He had all but given up. But the other consistent participant was an 84-year-old grandmother who wept and travailed continually in groaning prayer, contending for the church, for lost sons and daughters, and anyone else who happened to come to mind.

Not long after Dale attended this prayer gathering, a hippie in a Speedo, strung out on drugs and alcohol, came into a sparsely attended Sunday night meeting. He became so disruptive the pastor almost threw him out. Amazingly, he allowed him to stay. And long story short, the hippie got radically saved and delivered.

Not long after, the young man—no longer in a Speedo—asked the pastor if he would hold a special meeting on Monday evening, just for him and a few friends. Accommodations were reluctantly made for the extra service.

Turns out the hippie Speedo guy was extremely influential in Hollywood. The pastor had no idea. That Monday approximately a thousand of the man's closest friends attended the service! All ended up getting rocked for Jesus. And according to this apostolic evangelist taking a ferry from the end of the road into the Alaskan wilderness, who caught my ear by mentioning Jesus, that meeting became a spark for the entire Jesus revolution!

I want to see that spark released today, don't you? We are all contending. In many ways it may feel like you're at the end of the road. But a new Jesus revolution is just beyond! You and I are going to mark our children for the Lord, laying tracks in prayer for their turnaround.

And as this movement grows, an entire generation is going to meet the Lord at the threshold. It's turnaround time.

## TURNAROUND DECREE: "I WILL SAVE YOUR CHILDREN"

*For this is what the Lord says: "Even the captives of a mighty man will be taken, and the prey of a tyrant will be delivered; I will contend with the one who contends with you, and I will save your children" (Isaiah 49:25 CSB).*

*Father God, I am in awe of Your thoughtful, watchful care over me and my family, including the family of my future. In Your presence I now receive an aspect of Your Daniel 7:22 turnaround verdict in my favor: "I will save your children!"*

*I receive Isaiah 49:25 now as Your decree over my life. Accordingly, I decree that You now contend with the forces in the spiritual realm and the natural realm who contend with me. And that You now rescue my children from their grasp.*

RELEASING THE FORCE OF FAITH DECREES

*Father God, I dedicate my children—present and future—
to You, entrusting them into Your care. I call them out to
You by name (do this now). Father God, I also dedicate my
bloodline, my entire family tree, to You alone. Please grant
the annulment of all pacts and dedications made with
spiritual entities, as I have decided they must be owned by
the Lord Jesus Christ alone. I ask that all legal claims made
by these entities to own, influence, or harm my children
now be annulled by the body and blood of Jesus Christ.*

*According to Your decree I declare my children now enter
into complete freedom from their grasp. The captives of
the mighty tyrants are now rescued! And this deliverance
by the Lord Jesus Christ now manifests in every aspect
of their lives. Lord, I decree that the end of the road
now becomes a gateway to our new beginnings!*

*Lord, I thank You that You judge and make war. You
render Your decree and make war to uphold and enforce
it on earth. Accordingly, I thank You for now making war
to free my children! I call them fully back to You and fully
free to fulfill their covenant destiny, in Jesus's name!*

## SEVEN ON A SCROLL: RECEIVING AND DECLARING YOUR DECREE

1. Receive the decree of the Lord. What is the Spirit of God conveying to you, either by His Word, by His Spirit, or both?

2. Write the decree! So often decrees, dreams, and other communication from Holy Spirit are lost simply because we fail to record what we've received from Him.

3. Pray in the Spirit. When possible, worship and pray in the Spirit until you sense an unction to declare the decree He has given you.

4. Declare the decree! By speaking the decree, you are announcing to both the spirit realm and the earthly realm the directive of His governance.

5. Activate the angelic hosts. When you decree God's word, the angelic hosts are activated (see Psalm 103:20).

6. Train for the turnaround! This includes praying, repenting, and turning from any known sin that may give the enemy legal right to block the manifestation.

7. Keep watch over your decree. It must be "prayed through"!

## NOTE

1. Daniella J. Greenbaum, "Lighting Hanukkah Candles Under the Swastika's Shadow," *The New York Times*, December 12, 2017, https://www.nytimes.com/2017/12/12/opinion/happy -hanukkah-candles-swastikas.html; accessed January 20, 2023.

# 12

# CREATE HEAVENLY ATMOSPHERES IN YOUR HOME

by

*Brenda Runneman*

In a culture that aims to break down the family structure, we need to speak the right things over our lives and families. We need to verbally take authority over the power of the enemy that would attempt to bring any form of attack or destruction on our families and homes. We have the power to decree and put words into the atmosphere that will bring forth the manifestation of God's supernatural power upon our family life.

Our declaration of faith not only sets things in motion both spiritually and naturally, but it also builds our own faith that God is working out His purposes for our loved ones and will not let them fall. Our decree and declaration over our family also serves as a reminder to us that we should not slip into the temptation to speak negatively when it looks in the natural realm like things are turning out opposite of what we desire.

These decrees from my book, *Daily Decrees for Family Blessing and Breakthrough,* are tools to help families stand strong in the purposes of God so they can remain unified and experience prosperity and blessing. It will build faith in your spirit that whatever your family faces, God is working a miracle to turn it around for good. Through these declarations, you will also be reminding the enemy that your family, property, and possessions are off-limits and that your family will remain safe and secure! As you decree these words over your loved ones, you are setting nature in motion and establishing a bright future for those you love. It's time to declare blessing and breakthrough over your family!

## PEACE IN OUR HOME

### Declaration

Today we decree that our home is filled with God's unsurpassable peace. The atmosphere is saturated with tranquility and serenity. We rely on the Lord's peace, which provides a sense of assurance in our minds and emotions. We declare that we are relaxed and calm. We break the powers of agitation, mayhem, chaos, and disarray in the name of Jesus! We cast out any evil spirit that would bring disorder to the atmosphere. We declare that those who dwell in our home contribute to peace and do not give place to anything that would create turmoil. We speak that every person who enters our home is enveloped in heavenly peace. We say our home is a place where guests feel the Lord's supernatural rest upon them, and it opens the way for miracles in their lives. We speak great peace upon our home, in the mighty name of Jesus!

## Scripture

*Now the Lord of peace himself give you peace always by all means. The Lord be with you all* (2 Thessalonians 3:16 KJV).

## Word of Encouragement

Let's face it, life is busy and there are countless things that can disrupt the peace in our homes. Perhaps you work long hours and, as a result, responsibilities at home tend to fall behind, or maybe you have small children who need constant attention. In addition, there can be things like health issues and financial challenges that can rob our homes of peace. But the good news is the Lord is the giver of peace! He can extend a supernatural peace that can squelch the mayhem that would seek to invade your house. I want to encourage you to declare peace over your home. Along with that, work to create a peaceful home environment. Things like eliminating clutter, reducing excess noise, and increasing general organization can all contribute to improving peace. Remember, we do what we can both in the natural realm and the spiritual realm to walk in the peace the Lord wants us to experience. The key is not to allow life to rob the Lord's peace from your house!

## GLORY IN THE ATMOSPHERE

## Declaration

We decree that an atmosphere of God's glory floods our home. We speak and say that the presence of the Lord is everywhere. We call for the cloud of God's *Shekinah* glory to invade every room and crevice of our house. May every person who enters here be affected by the glory of the Lord. Because of the atmosphere of glory, we receive the goodness of the Lord, even as Moses saw God's goodness when he encountered the glory. We take authority over any demonic interference that would squelch the atmosphere of glory. We prophesy that in the glory we are changed, healed, and delivered. We submit ourselves to whatever the Holy Spirit wants to accomplish. We avail ourselves of spending time in the Lord's presence, and we allow the glory to rest upon our lives. Lord, we thank You that Your glory permeates us and is welcome in our house. Like Moses, we ask to see Your glory and we want to experience it daily in our home!

## Scripture

*And he said, I beseech thee, shew me thy glory* (Exodus 33:18 KJV).

## Word of Encouragement

The encounter between God and Moses in Exodus 33 is undoubtedly one of the most impactful biblical encounters between God and a human being. It was an expression of a man who wanted to be entirely immersed in the awesome presence of Almighty God. Moses' yearning was so intense that he literally begged for the Lord to allow His glory to be visible. In other words, Moses wanted to see God with his eyes!

Today we are not much different from Moses in our desire to see the Lord. Yes, we want to see Him with our eyes, but we also want to experience Him in every aspect of our being. We express this desire by saying, "I want to experience the glory!" In that, we want our homes to be a place where the glory of the Lord is present and felt by those who live in and enter our home. We want our homes to be a place where people come and literally sense the Lord.

If you want to have the Lord's glory in the atmosphere of your house, then it needs to be cherished and protected. Be careful not to allow things that squelch the glory or interfere with it. Consider the things you read or watch on TV and electronic devices. Ensure that your actions do not hinder the presence of His glory. Then make the point to invite the Lord's glory to have its welcomed place around you on a regular basis. Ask the Lord for the atmosphere of glory to be in your home!

## AN ATMOSPHERE FOR MIRACLES

## Declaration

We decree that our home is an atmosphere where miracles operate and manifest regularly. We declare that we receive divine experiences and supernatural encounters from Heaven. We receive manifestations that turn impossible situations around and bring blessing and surprises. People get healed in our home and receive instantaneous miracles. We declare the manifestation of miracles, signs, and wonders flows freely. We say that signs follow the Word of God that is spoken and preached in our home. We invite the supernatural presence of the Lord to take up residence here. We break the power of all hindrances, unbelief, and religious spirits that would discount miracles, and we prophesy that our minds are open and receptive to the supernatural move of God. We are a family who creates the atmosphere of miracles in our home, in Jesus' name!

## Scripture

*And the disciples went everywhere and preached, and the Lord worked through them, confirming what they said by many miraculous signs* (Mark 16:20 NLT).

## Word of Encouragement

Many believers do not fully understand the miraculous side of God, particularly when it comes to receiving miracles in their own lives. People often do not progress beyond the realm of guessing what God will do about their situation, or if and when they will experience the miracle they're desiring. The age-old question of why some people receive a miracle and others do not remains difficult to answer because not all situations are exactly the same. However, we *do* know this—we *can* create an environment that sets the atmosphere for miracles. We see this in the ministry of Jesus. People who received miracles from Him were in a place of faith for such; they were anticipating that they would receive (see Matthew 8:13; Mark 5:34; 9:23).

On the flip side, when Jesus came to Nazareth, He was unable to do any mighty works because of their unbelief (see Mark 6:5). They resisted and analyzed Jesus' miracle-working power and, as a result, they did not receive. We must be people who create an atmosphere that is receptive to God's miracle-working power. We do so by believing for it, not by analyzing it logically and ultimately rejecting it, like the people of Nazareth. Instead, talk about miracles in your home. When you pray, tell the Lord how much you believe in His miracle power. Build your faith on the Word of God that reveals how willing He is to exercise His miraculous nature on your behalf. Declare that your home is filled with miracles, and always speak accordingly. Also, avoid unbelief and speaking negatively when circumstances seem adverse and it doesn't appear that God will step in. Your home *is* a place for miracles!

## A No-Fly Zone!

### Declaration

We decree that our house is a no-fly zone to the operations of the enemy! Just as the children of Israel were separated by God from the plague of flies that came upon the Egyptians, so are we protected from every plague of the enemy. No evil forces, plots, plans, or works of demonic spirits can access the premises of our house. We say that the doors to our home are never entered by any entity that is in opposition to God. We break the power of any spells, incantations, or hexes from any witch, warlock, or worker of divination, in Jesus' name. We prophesy that no plague, pestilence, accident, tragedy, calamity, mischief, or mayhem is allowed to enter here, in the name of Jesus! All forces of darkness and evil must cease and desist from any maneuver or operation being attempted against this household. Our house is protected by the blood of Jesus that is upon its doorposts. A divine hedge surrounds our property and the angels of the Most High are standing guard. We live in safety and peace because our house is a no-fly zone to the enemy!

### Scripture

> *And I will sever in that day the land of Goshen, in which my people dwell, that no swarms of flies shall be there; to the end thou mayest know that I am the Lord in the midst of the earth* (Exodus 8:22 KJV).

## Word of Encouragement

When God sent the ten plagues upon Egypt, the Bible doesn't specify that the Lord separated the Israelites who lived in Goshen from the Egyptians until the fourth plague, the swarm of flies. While this isn't to say the plagues were *in* Goshen, it's not clear whether the Israelites working among the Egyptians weren't equally affected by the first three plagues. But we know that when the flies came, God brought a divine separation between the Egyptians and the children of Israel. This is important—it helps us to see that we can trust God to separate His people from the world. Part of that separation includes a separation of favor, protection, and increase. Have confidence today that the Lord is separating you and your family from all the mayhem in the world. Declare today and every day that your home is a "no-fly zone" to all the enemy's operations!

## STRIFE IS BROKEN!

### Declaration

Today we break the power of strife over our home and our family! We decree our home is an environment where strife has no place and no voice. We rebuke all demonic powers that would create contention, bickering, quarrels, and altercations, in the name of Jesus. We say that we refuse to be lured into strife-filled conversations and situations. We declare that anger, contention, touchiness, grouchiness, temper tantrums, and flare-ups are not allowed in our home. We prophesy that we are a family who controls our emotions, words, and attitudes and we submit them to the lordship of Jesus Christ. We say strife is replaced with patience and self-control. We do not stir up strife with our actions, and we choose to create a home that is strife-free and contention-free. We prophesy that in our family and home the power of strife is broken!

## Scripture

*A hot-tempered person stirs up strife, but the slow to anger calms a dispute* (Proverbs 15:18 NASB).

## Word of Encouragement

No one enjoys contention or contentious conversations. Resolving differences considerately is very different from allowing strife to run freely through your household. Most strife arises when those involved have a difficult time controlling feelings, attitudes, and the like. It usually results in sharp tones of voice, sarcastic comments, or rude body language. Strife must be a bigger problem than we'd like to think, because so many Scripture verses, particularly in the New Testament, address avoiding strife and contention. When we realize that being a strife-filled, contentious person doesn't please God, we know that we need to avoid strife at all costs. Strife not only hurts those around us, it robs our day of joy and fulfillment. Demonic spirits love to stir up strife, so we must not to become ensnared by them! A key to learning how to be a person devoid of strife is to speak over yourself that the power of strife will not be allowed to rule over you or take control of the environment in your house. Declaring strife is broken will remind you not to stir up strife when the opportunity arises, but rather to do the opposite and maintain peace!

## Financial Provision and Increase

### Declaration

We decree that we live in a constant place of financial provision and increase. We live under that continual fountain of heavenly supply. We say that each year our finances grow to another level of increase and abundance. We break the power of decrease and decline, in the name of Jesus! We break the power of bankruptcy, deficiency, and depletion. We prophesy that financial distress and crisis of every kind is replaced with financial contentment and stability. We say that we receive regular boosts and raises and that no bill goes unpaid. We will always have more than enough, excess, and overflow, and every need we will ever have shall be provided for, in Jesus' name!

### Scripture

*The blessing of the Lord, it maketh rich, and he addeth no sorrow with it* (Proverbs 10:22 KJV).

### Word of Encouragement

Many believers have a hard time envisioning God providing them financial sufficiency that goes above and beyond just getting by. In fact, too often people are content to live well below what the Lord really wants for them. But consider the many ways that financial deficiency is not a blessing! It creates stress and hardship, yet many believers simply accept it. In saying this, some will automatically retort, "Yes, but the apostle Paul encouraged that we should know how to live both in sufficiency and also in need!" (see Philippians 4:12). While it's true that we need to maintain the same position of faith in times when lack tries to arise, Paul wasn't implying that we are to be accepting of lack. He was teaching that in all times, we must keep our faith engaged for a breakthrough and not give up when we face difficulties.

God wants us to experience constant financial provision, and that is what we should set our faith upon. Jesus said He came to give life and life *more* abundantly (see John 10:10). Of course, this verse doesn't only refer to financial provision, but it's definitely part of the package! Include financial provision in your daily declarations. Begin to see yourself on a constant track of increase and refuse to accept decrease and lack. If the Lord wants you to be supplied, then the key is to get in agreement with God and expect financial provision!

## OVERWHELMING PRESENCE

### Declaration

We decree that the overwhelming presence of the Lord rests in our home. His presence causes us to experience joy and to rejoice every day. The Lord's presence in our lives and home transcends every circumstance and situation. We cannot hide from the Lord's presence and He is with us wherever we go. His presence upon us breaks the power of all manner of bondage and strongholds. We prophesy that no form of demonic oppression can reside in our home because the presence of the Lord drives it out. Just as the mountains melt like wax at the presence of the Lord, so do any obstacles in our lives. We declare that we experience complete freedom and liberty because of the presence of the Lord. We come into His presence with rejoicing and singing. We constantly search for ways to experience His presence in our lives. We decree that the overwhelming presence of the Lord is upon our family now!

## Scripture

> *Thou wilt shew me the path of life: in thy presence is fulness of joy; at thy right hand there are pleasures for evermore* (Psalm 16:11 KJV).

## Word of Encouragement

There are countless, wonderful attributes about the presence of God, and the Bible promises many benefits to those who experience it. There is joy, liberty, peace, and divine power in His presence. The Bible says the mountains literally melt like wax in the presence of the Lord (see Psalm 97:5); this means that nothing can withstand His presence. For the person who desires God's presence, it will destroy the demonic and also bring hope and deliverance. In our lives and homes, we must constantly pursue the things that invite the Lord's presence. Obviously, consistent prayer and time reading the Bible will bring His presence into manifestation. Attending church is also a key way to experience the presence of the Lord as you are surrounded by other believers in the atmosphere of worship. And last, tell the Lord how much you want His presence in your life and family! He wants to hear you express your desire for Him. Developing a daily consciousness of the Lord's presence will cause you to experience His overwhelming presence in your life, in your home, and upon your family.

## ANGELS SURROUND US

### Declaration

Today we decree that the angels of the Lord surround our home and family. They stand watch to ensure that we experience no tragedy or harm. We prophesy that we are under the charge of the royal guard of the hosts of Heaven. They are keeping us safe and secure. We speak that no member in our family can be hurt or injured in any way because of the presence of angels. We also say that they stand watch around the perimeter of our home and around every piece of property that we own. No thief, attacker, burglar, or plunderer can access our dwelling because the angels of the Lord are on duty and fighting on our behalf. The angels stand as ministers for us as the children of the Most High. Because Heaven's ministering servants are at work, we can live in peace and complete security. Our family is surrounded by His angels!

### Scripture

> *For he shall give his angels charge over thee, to keep thee in all thy ways. They shall bear thee up in their hands, lest thou dash thy foot against a stone* (Psalm 91:11-12 KJV).

### Word of Encouragement

One of the most comforting truths and promises of Scripture is the knowledge that the Lord's angels are surrounding His people. Realizing that angels are on duty around you and around your children and property is important. If we truly understood the role of angels, it would encourage us not to speak from fear or speak negatively. Sometimes we speak wrongly because we forget that not only is God at work in our situation, but He has commissioned angels to work for us. In fact, the Bible says they are ministers specifically for God's children (see Hebrews 1:14). We must also remember that angels respond to God's Word (see Psalm 103:20). That's why speaking negatively can hinder the work of angels. We want the angels to respond to God's Word coming from our mouth. We don't want to hinder them because we are speaking words of fear or unbelief. Reminding yourself each day about the presence and work of angels around you will bring comfort. It will cause you to be assured that not only you, but each member of your family, will be safe and secure because they are surrounded by His angels!

## No Fear Here!

### Declaration

We decree that our family is free from all forms of fear. We prophesy that fear has no place in our home or upon any member of our family. We command all evil spirits of fear to leave, in the name of Jesus! We declare that *all forms* of fear must also go. We break the power of worry, anxiety, fretfulness, insecurity, panic, dread, and terror. Our household is off-limits to fear. We refuse to give in or submit to fear, and we prophesy that we are a family who chooses to stand up in faith in every situation. We are free from fear because the Lord is helping us and giving us His strength. We have no fear of people, for the Lord is our help and refuge. The Lord is our light and our salvation, and we have no need to be afraid. We declare fear is replaced with faith and confidence. All forms of fear are reversed and replaced with assurance, calm, cheer, and peace. We are fear-free, in Jesus' name!

## Scripture

*Fear thou not; for I am with thee: be not dismayed; for I am thy God: I will strengthen thee; yea, I will help thee; yea, I will uphold thee with the right hand of my righteousness* (Isaiah 41:10 KJV).

## Word of Encouragement

If there is one encouragement Scripture repeats again and again, it's the encouragement not to fear. Consider how many times the Lord or His angels gave His people the admonition, "Fear not!" What we can glean from this is that it's tempting to fall into fear. If we're not careful, we can look at the circumstances in the world or in our own lives and let fear creep in. We must resist the temptation to fear because fear is a debilitating enemy. It can paralyze you from normal life, prevent you from carrying out your purpose, and keep you imprisoned—both physically and emotionally.

We counter the enemy of fear with the Word of God. Have ready in your arsenal a list of verses that serve as a continual reminder of why you need not live in fear. When fear tries to arise, resist it and verbally command it to leave, in the authority of Jesus' name. Don't dwell on fearful thoughts or they will escalate. Don't allow it to stay for a single moment! Resist it immediately and command every fearful thought to leave your mind. Declare every single day, "There is no fear here!"

## GENERATIONAL CURSES BOUND!

### Declaration

We decree that all generational curses are bound and eradicated from our family. We prophesy that the sins of prior generations are broken and no longer influence our bloodline. We declare that all ideas, habits, patterns, and practices that are not of God are unable to operate in our family line. We break the power of any prior curses spoken through the spirit of witchcraft, and we prophesy that these curses are severed and shredded, in the name of Jesus! As a family, we practice habits and routines that are the opposite of the curse. We live and operate according to the will of God and His Word. We make it our intention to look for ways to increase the blessing upon our family and in our home. We declare that going forward, we step into a new and fresh generational blessing that shall be manifest upon our bloodline, both now and in the future. We declare that we are richly blessed because the curse upon our generation is broken, in Jesus' name!

### Scripture

*May the Lord richly bless both you and your children* (Psalm 115:14 NLT).

### Word of Encouragement

People talk about generational curses because they recognize the fact that many habits, strongholds, and sins are passed down from generation to generation. The Bible reveals that under the Old Testament, God will hold the responsibility of people's sins upon their children even to the third and fourth generations (see Exodus 20:5). This isn't because God is unjust and makes our children pay for our wrongs. It is revealing that what we choose to do today, our children will often repeat, and therefore they will end up paying the price for those choices. The good news is, generational patterns or "curses" can be broken! The Bible says Jesus was made the curse for us (see Galatians 3:13). He took the curse upon Himself so we don't have to bear it. In Christ, we have the ability to break the power of generational patterns, first by repenting of our own sins, then asking God to help us not to repeat the bad habits or patterns of generations before us. Then last, we can command the power of any evil spirits influencing these patterns to be broken, in the name of Jesus! Declare today your family is free from the generational curse and God's rich blessing is upon you and your children!

## WE WILL SERVE THE LORD

### Declaration

Today we declare that all who live in our home serve the Lord. We prophesy that each member of this household honors God in word, action, and deed. We are a family who gives the Lord the place of supreme rule, and we choose to uphold His Word and commandments. His name shall always be reverenced under our roof. We speak words of praise and esteem about the Lord. We speak that in this home the Lord is high and lifted up, and His presence fills every room! We say that no antichrist spirit is able to operate in this house. We break the power of any opposing spirit or influence, and we close the door to all things that dishonor our God. We decree that the banner written upon the doorposts of this house is, "As for me and my house, we serve the Lord!"

## Scripture

*And if it seem evil unto you to serve the Lord, choose you this day whom ye will serve; whether the gods which your fathers served that were on the other side of the flood, or the gods of the Amorites, in whose land ye dwell: but as for me and my house, we will serve the Lord* (Joshua 24:15 KJV).

## Word of Encouragement

One of the most important things a family can do is decide that their home will be a place where God is honored. This means that anything that would dishonor the Lord is not allowed access to the premises; all that is said and done carries the Lord's honor upon it. Moses taught the children of Israel that they were to teach their children to praise and honor God in everything they did. This was not to be a one-time decision. It was something they acknowledged in an ongoing way. There is so much in our culture that dishonors God today and, over time, it can be easy to unintentionally allow things to creep into our homes that are in opposition to the Lord. Regularly making the verbal declaration—that your house will be one that gives God the preeminence in everything—will ensure your home remains free of the things that would bring dishonor to Him!

## TIME FOR TOGETHERNESS

### Declaration

Today we declare that our home is filled with oneness, togetherness, unity, and fellowship. Our home is characterized by a closeness and affection between all who live and visit here. We love to be together, talk, interact, and communicate with one another. We are a family that enjoys fun activities without distraction or interruption. We say that nothing can disrupt our family time and the closeness we share in this home. We break the power of all evil spirits that would come to separate, divide, distract, or invade our togetherness, in Jesus' name! We prophesy that we have our schedules, plans, and activities in order so that an atmosphere of unity thrives and we can spend time together without disruption or distraction. We say that we are a household of togetherness and we are a family of closeness!

### Scripture

*Behold, how good and how pleasant it is for brethren to dwell together in unity!* (Psalm 133:1 KJV)

### Word of Encouragement

If you are like many families, you already know the challenges that can arise to keep you from spending quality time with your loved ones. You also know there are countless things that can creep in to create separation until everyone is so busy doing their own thing that they're doing nothing together. Family togetherness is the quest of nearly every family that exists, and it's something to be fought for and protected. Make it a goal to develop quality family time, while simultaneously considering what you can eliminate that might disrupt family togetherness. Too often a sense of closeness isn't just built by what we do; it's also built by what we remove.

For example, too many hours at work will eventually take its toll on family time. It's also important to consider that a sense of togetherness can be easily increased through simple, meaningful, and regular conversation. Phone calls, kind notes, and thoughtful gestures all lead to feelings of closeness. Lastly, avoid speaking words of division or expressing continual feelings of frustration. Instead, declare togetherness and allow it to permeate the atmosphere of your home!

## RESTFUL SLEEP

### Declaration

We decree that every member of our household and family experiences nights of restful sleep. We prophesy an atmosphere of complete peace and tranquility in our home that enables us to sleep soundly every night. We break the power of all sleep disorders, insomnia, sleep apnea, restlessness, discomfort, nightmares, anxieties, fears, and imbalances, in the name of Jesus. We declare no evil spirit can interject itself while our family is asleep. We reject and resist anything that would disrupt our sleep, and we prophesy that our regular sleep schedule is well-established and stays on track. We decree that we have the wisdom to create an environment that promotes rest and comfort. We prophesy that we have divine dreams, heavenly visitations, and visions while we sleep. We ask the Lord to give us restful sleep so that every day we awake refreshed, rejuvenated, and filled with renewed energy! We say that every member of our family is able to sleep peacefully and that we experience continual nights of uninterrupted, restful sleep!

## Scripture

*It is vain for you to rise up early, to sit up late, to eat the bread of sorrows: for so he giveth his beloved sleep* (Psalm 127:2 KJV).

## Word of Encouragement

With entire medical studies, industries, and countless products dedicated to the sleep experience, it's undisputed that a good night's rest is paramount to our quality of life. A lack of proper sleep leads to medical problems, depression, and an overall lack of productivity, just to name a few. It's important to do what you can in the natural to help promote sleep. Keeping a schedule and regular bedtime where possible, creating the right atmosphere, and proper bedding are all things that help promote rest. However, sometimes sleep is interrupted by the forces of the enemy. Satan loves to attack people when they are sleeping by invading them with fears, nightmares, or medically related problems that disrupt their sleep. What we must know is that God *gives* His beloved sleep. Just as the enemy can try to interrupt sleep, the Lord can bring a supernatural sleep upon you. Before retiring at night, declare that you will have a night of restful and uninterrupted sleep and nothing shall interfere with it, in Jesus' name.

## Understanding and Compassion Fill My House

### Declaration

We decree that our home is a place where compassion is exemplified. We respond and react to everything through the eye of the Lord's compassion. We declare that every person who enters our home senses the care and love of God that discerns their needs. We prophesy that as a family, our hearts are filled with kindness, generosity, and consideration for others. In our home, we have hearts that understand one another's needs. We declare that we are saturated by the supernatural compassion of God that deeply moves us and results in miracles! We say that any attitude that is opposite of God's compassion has no place in our hearts. We reject any spirit that would cause us to become selfishly intolerant or inconsiderate. We say that understanding and compassion fill our home, our lives, and our family, in Jesus' name!

### Scripture

*And Jesus went forth, and saw a great multitude, and was moved with compassion toward them, and he healed their sick* (Matthew 14:14 KJV).

### Word of Encouragement

When challenges in dealing with others arise, sometimes it's difficult to understand where another person is coming from. One of the hardest things to master is being able to put ourselves in someone else's shoes. It's probably one of the reasons people easily jump toward criticism rather than being able to pause and see someone else's position on things. Jesus, just after the beheading of John the Baptist in Matthew 14, was able to see the needs of the multitude. In the middle of His own sorrow following a deep loss, He discerned the need of the people. He was able to set His own needs aside and allow Himself to be governed by a compassion for those around Him. He didn't just muster up the compassion to minister to the people, either. The Bible says He was *moved* with compassion. This means, within Him was a deep yearning and care for what concerned them. And notice that His compassion resulted in miracles and healing! Compassion and healing go together. There is something special released in our home and family when we choose to be governed by the Lord's compassion!

## PRODIGALS COMING HOME

### Declaration

We decree that prodigal, backslidden, and wayward children and family members are coming home. We prophesy that revelation from Heaven comes upon them and they will make a sudden shift in their thinking and begin to turn to God in a supernatural way. We speak divine, heavenly revelation over them that causes them to miraculously change direction. We declare that the eyes of every one of our family members who have strayed away from the Lord are open to truth. We break the power of every deceiving, seducing spirit that is pulling them away, in Jesus' name! We say the laborers are placed in their paths who will lead them toward truth. We prophesy that they have encounters and experiences that lead them to the Lord. We decree their hearts and minds are softened to truth and that all hard-heartedness is broken by the power and love of God. We say that any relationships, friendships, alliances, or soul ties that would hold them in bondage are broken, in Jesus' name! We declare the prodigals are coming home!

## Scripture

*For this my son was dead, and is alive again; he was lost, and is found. And they began to be merry* (Luke 15:24 KJV).

## Word of Encouragement

There are few believers who haven't experienced the heartbreak that comes when a family member or loved one drifts away from the Lord. We feel this because a life without Jesus is one that eventually results in ruin, both now and in eternity. The consequences are high and, therefore, we have great joy and peace when our loved ones are serving the Lord. One of the most valuable things we can do for those who have gone wayward is pray. It's sometimes tempting to try and win them through constant pressuring. However, pressuring, nagging, and "preaching" can often make them more hardened. This doesn't mean we never present truth, because we do need to be sensitive to the Holy Spirit when He tells us to speak. What we can't do is continue speaking to them out of fear and frustration. When it comes to prodigals, we must use our faith. Our declaration for them during our times of prayer is very powerful. Things are moving that you may not necessarily see, but you can trust that God is at work and prodigals are coming home!

## No Fear of the Future

### Declaration

We declare that, as a family, we have no fear or dread of what the future holds. We look forward to what lies ahead because we are confident that the Lord has a good plan for us. Our family does not base our view of the future on our past experiences. We base our view of the future on the Word of God and its promises! We declare that no negativity, bad experiences, or traumatic events can follow us into our future. We break the power of any tracking evil spirit that would use the negativity of the past to form our mindsets and beliefs, in Jesus' name. We break the power of every form of fear and inhibition about what tomorrow holds. We are confident that the future of all our family members, loved ones, and descendants shall be protected and secured by the Lord's Almighty hand. We prophesy that our future shall be bright, excellent, fulfilling, and marked by joyful experiences. Our family stands in assurance and faith that everything that lies ahead shall be carefully governed by the Lord and all shall be well for us. We decree we have no fear of the future, in Jesus' name!

### Scripture

> *Therefore do not worry about tomorrow, for tomorrow will worry about itself. Each day has enough trouble of its own* (Matthew 6:34 NIV).

### Word of Encouragement

With all the uncertainty in today's world, more people—including believers—are skeptical about tomorrow. However, we must remind ourselves that Jesus emphatically told us not to fret about tomorrow. He even said that today carries enough of its own challenges, so we certainly shouldn't be wringing our hands about something that hasn't happened! The problem with worrying about tomorrow is that it's a mirage of sorts. It's a concern over something that hasn't taken place, and by worrying about the future we simply borrow trouble unnecessarily. A famous philosopher once said, "My life has been filled with terrible misfortune, most of which never happened!" This is what worrying about the future is—expecting misfortunes that will probably not happen. We need to obey what Jesus taught and put the concerns about the future of our family, our children, and our lives aside. We must have faith about the future, not fear of the future!

## Blessing upon Our Children

### Declaration

We decree that the children in our family are blessed. We command a supernatural blessing upon all the children in our immediate family and upon those of our loved ones. We say that the generation of the upright comes under divine blessing and nothing shall interfere with it. We prophesy that our children are shielded against anything in the current culture that would try to persuade, entice, or influence them with anything opposed to the Word of God. We prophesy that our children and our children's children shall serve the Lord and not depart from Him. We break the power of any evil spirit that would attempt to harm, abuse, or afflict them, in the Name of Jesus. We say the angels of the Lord's royal guard shall stand watch over our children and destroy the power of any attacker. Our children walk in health, protection, prosperity, and security. We say that our children are a heritage from the Lord and they shall fulfill their divine purpose for their generation!

## Scripture

*Praise ye the Lord. Blessed is the man that feareth the Lord, that delighteth greatly in his commandments. His seed shall be mighty upon earth: the generation of the upright shall be blessed* (Psalm 112:1-2 KJV).

## Word of Encouragement

One thing that moves the heart of any parent or grandparent is knowing that their children are blessed. Good parents want nothing more than for their children to turn out well. Therefore, we typically do all we can to ensure they are provided for, live in a secure environment, are given love, taught responsibility for living, and so on. As Christian parents, we also want to ensure their spiritual upbringing by teaching them God's Word, praying with them, and involving them in church. Yet another important aspect that could be overlooked are the words and declarations we speak over our children. Like anything else in life, what we say affects our outcome. What we say over our children is a catalyst in determining their destiny. Getting in agreement with what God says about the children in your family is one of the greatest things you can do to ensure their future. Agree with God and decree that the generation of the upright is blessed!

# DECREE YOUR BREAKTHROUGH FAITH TODAY

*For by grace you have been saved through faith, and that not of yourselves; it is the gift of God, not of works, lest anyone should boast. For we are His workmanship, created in Christ Jesus for good works, which God prepared beforehand that we should walk in them* (Ephesians 2:8-10 NKJV).

I celebrate the miracles, signs, and wonders that a life of breakthrough faith produces—otherwise, I would not have written this book. My driving prayer over this project is that the body of Christ would begin to walk out a lifestyle of consistent miraculous power, not just occasional victory. But to what end? I want to see Jesus Christ high and lifted up so that all would know He is the one true God. He is the only way to eternal salvation. And He is our invitation to a life of purpose and significance here on earth.

*Jesus is alive.*

*He is not a concept.*

*He is not one among many gods.*

*Jesus is God.*

*There is no other name under Heaven by which man can be saved from sin.*

*Jesus is the Savior.*

*By nature, mankind is sinful.*

*Our natural bent is toward sin and rebellion.*

*We could not save ourselves from this drive toward evil tendencies.*

*We were incapable of becoming right with God.*

*This is why God Himself came to the earth as Jesus Christ.*

*He lived the life that you and I could not live—one of absolute perfection.*

*He died the death that you and I deserved to die—and even if we had died that same death, our humanness would have prevented our sacrifice from doing anything about the sin problem.*

*Jesus's blood was perfect and holy and sinless—it brought forgiveness for your sin and my sin. For the sins of the entire world. All of the wrong. All of the rebellion. All of the pride. All of the anger. All of the lust. All of the hatred. Every thought, action, and attitude in rebellion toward God was taken care of at the cross.*

We simply need to receive the free gift that God provided through Jesus. *This is how we receive breakthrough faith!* If you have already made Jesus Christ your Lord and Savior, I have good news for you: you already have breakthrough faith living inside of you. However, if you have never invited Jesus to come into your life, forgive your sins, give you a fresh start, and fill you with the Holy Spirit to live out the supernatural life-style we just explored, I want to give you the opportunity right here, right now. It is so simple. You can just pray with me:

*Jesus, thank You for living a perfect life. I couldn't do it.*

*Thank You, Jesus, for dying the perfect death,*
*offering complete forgiveness for my sins.*

*Father, I confess that my sin, my wrong, my*
*rebellion—it all deserves death, for the Bible*
*says that the soul that sins shall die.*

*This is what causes me to feel unworthy before You, the*
*Holy God. But I don't need to stay this way. You made*
*it possible for me to stand righteous before You!*

*Thank You, Jesus, for taking my place and dying*
*the death that I deserved. You took upon Yourself*
*all of my sin—past, present, and future.*

*I am forgiven. I am clean. I am shameless.*
*I am guilt-free. Thank You, Jesus.*

*And finally, thank You for filling me with Your Holy*
*Spirit. You forgave my sin so that I could spend eternity*
*in Heaven with You, but also so that I could be filled with*
*Your Presence and power here on earth. I want to see*
*Your Kingdom bring freedom, healing, and breakthrough*
*so that all would know that Jesus Christ is alive!*

If you prayed this simple prayer, I believe the Holy Spirit performed an utterly supernatural work in your heart. Jesus Christ saved you from your sin, made you a child of God, and filled you with the Holy Spirit. You are now what they call "born again." You are a Christian. You have a room reserved in Heaven and are empowered with breakthrough faith for your mission on earth.

Above all, I pray that every breakthrough you experience fuels your passion and pursuit for this Jesus, to know Him more, to worship Him more deeply, and to boldly declare His glorious Gospel to the nations, starting with your own sphere of influence.

# About the Author & Contributors

## Larry Sparks

Larry Sparks has been in ministry for more than two decades. He serves as publisher for Destiny Image and travels internationally, teaching on revival, awakening and Pentecostal Fire. He received a Master of Divinity from Regent University in Church History and Renewal. Larry hosts regular programs on *God TV* and the *It's Supernatural Network*. He lives in Texas with his wife, Mercedes, and daughter, Liberty. Larry presently serves on the Apostolic Council of Prophetic Elders (ACPE) under the direction of Cindy Jacobs. He is the author of multiple books, including *Pentecostal Fire*, *Ask for the Rain* and *Accessing the Greater Glory*. The opening three chapters of *The Force of Faith Decrees* were taken from his book, *Breakthrough Faith—Living a Life Where Anything Is Possible*.

## BILL JOHNSON

BILL JOHNSON is the Senior Leader of Bethel Church in Redding, California. He is a fifth-generation pastor with a rich heritage in the Holy Spirit. The present move of God has brought Bill into a deeper understanding of the phrase "on earth as it is in heaven." Bill and the Bethel Church family have taken on this theme for life and ministry, where healing and miracles are normal. He is co-founder of Bethel School of Supernatural Ministry (BSSM). Bethel's apostolic network has crossed denominational lines in building relationships that enable church leaders to walk in both purity and power. Bill and his wife, Beni (who passed into Heaven in 2022), and their three children and spouses are all involved in full-time ministry. They have eleven grandchildren. Bill Johnson's chapter in *The Force of Faith Decrees* was taken from his book, *God Is Good—He's Better Than You Think*.

## JODIE HUGHES

JODIE AND BEN HUGHES are the founders of Pour It Out Ministries and have been in ministry together for more than twenty years. They, along with their adult daughter, Keely, travel full time around the world as Revivalists, with an emphasis on breakthrough, prophetic declaration, healing, and preaching the gospel with miracles, signs, and wonders following in their personal lives and ministry endeavors. Ministering as a family imparts great hope and relatability to many.

They are known for hosting the eighteen-month Pineapple Revival in Australia, which saw many thousands come from around the world to attend. As well as being full-time itinerant Revivalists and prophets, they have pastored and planted several churches, trained thousands of ministry students in their schools, recorded worship albums, and authored prophetic insight articles and blogs. Jodie pioneered and leads Mentor Me, an international online mentoring program, and regularly releases prophetic words and mentoring wisdom. She is an engaging speaker and influencer known for being real, inspiring hope, imparting contagious hunger, and transferable revival fire. Originally from Australia, they are based in Texas, USA. Visit their website at: www.pouritout.org. Jodie Hughes' chapter in *The Force of Faith Decrees* was taken from her book, *The King's Decrees—Throne Room Declarations That Release Supernatural Answers to Prayer.*

## TIM SHEETS

DR. TIM SHEETS is an apostle, pastor, author, and founder of AwakeningNow Prayer Network based in Middletown, Ohio, at the Oasis Church, which he has pastored for 36 years. He travels and ministers across the nation and other countries. He can be reached at: @TimDSheets (Twitter); Tim Sheets Ministries (Facebook); timsheets.org; oasiswired.org; awakeningnowprayernetwork.com. Tim Sheets' chapter in *The Force of Faith Decrees* was taken from his book, *Planting the Heavens—Releasing the Authority of the Kingdom Through Your Words, Prayers, and Declarations.*

## Tommy and Miriam Evans

Tommy and Miriam Evans travel locally, nationally, and internationally holding revival meetings, miracle services, and supernatural school intensives for inviting churches and conferences. Along with their itinerant ministry, Tommy and Miriam are senior leaders of Trinity Church's Saturday Night Awakening Service in Cedar Hill, Texas, where they hold weekly revival meetings. They co-founded Mandate of Hope Ministries, a global itinerant ministry organized to function on a local, national, and international scale by preaching and teaching the Gospel of Jesus Christ through the power of the Holy Spirit. Along with their ministry, Miriam and Tommy serve as members of the Apostolic Council of Prophetic Elders with Generals International. Tommy, Miriam, and their five children, Kathryn, Madison, Lauren, Benjamin, and Levi, live in the Dallas/Fort Worth Texas area. The Evans' chapter in *The Force of Faith Decrees* was taken from their book, *Decrees That Unlock Heaven's Power—Prayers and Declarations That Release Miracles, Breakthrough, and Supernatural Answers.*

## Robert Henderson

Robert Henderson is a global, apostolic leader who operates in revelation and impartation. His teaching empowers the body of Christ to see the hidden truths of Scripture clearly and apply them for breakthrough results. Driven by a mandate to disciple nations through writing and speaking, Robert travels extensively around the globe, teaching on the apostolic, the Kingdom of God, the "Seven Mountains," and most notably, the Courts of Heaven. He and Mary have been married for more than 40 years. They have six children and five grandchildren. Together they are enjoying life in beautiful Midlothian, Texas. Robert Henderson's chapter in *The Force of Faith Decrees* was taken from his book, *Prayers and Declarations That Open the Courts of Heaven*.

## JENNIFER LECLAIRE

JENNIFER LECLAIRE is an internationally recognized author, apostolic-prophetic voice to her generation, and conference speaker. Jennifer is senior leader of Awakening House of Prayer in Fort Lauderdale, Florida, founder of the Ignite Network and founder of the Awakening Prayer Hubs prayer movement. She formerly served as the first female editor of *Charisma* magazine.

Jennifer is a prolific author who has written over 50 books. Beyond her frequent appearances on the Elijah List, Jennifer writes a popular prophetic columns, The Plumb Line. She has been interviewed on numerous media outlets including *USA Today, BBC, CBN, The Alan Colmes Show, Bill Martinez Live, Babbie's House, Atlanta Live,* and Sid Roth's *It's Supernatural,* as well as serving as an analyst for Rolling Thunder Productions on a Duck Dynasty special presentation. Jennifer also sits on the media advisory board of the Hispanic Israel Leadership Coalition. Jennifer LeClaire's chapter in *The Force of Faith Decrees* was taken from her book, *Victory Decrees—Daily Prophetic Strategies for Spiritual Warfare Victory.*

## JON AND JOLENE HAMILL

JON AND JOLENE HAMILL are passionate followers of Jesus Christ. Based in Washington, DC, they have witnessed firsthand the power of biblical equipping, watchman prayer, and prophetic ministry to catalyze God's intended turnaround. They are popular speakers nationally and internationally and are active in media, producing an online blog that reaches many thousands weekly. The founders of Lamplighter Ministries, Jon and Jolene have authored four books. The Hammill's chapter in *The Force of Faith Decrees* was taken from their book, *Turnaround Decrees—Disrupt the Enemy's Plans and Shift Your Circumstance into Breakthrough.*

## BRENDA KUNNEMAN

BRENDA KUNNEMAN is co-founder of One Voice Ministries and pastors Lord of Hosts Church with her husband. Brenda is a captivating preacher with a powerful prophetic anointing. She preaches a cutting-edge Kingdom message and lives have been changed by specific prophecies for both individuals and churches. With a ministry of impartation and deliverance many have been healed and set free. Brenda ministers in conferences and churches and has made several television appearances both nationally and internationally. She also ministers with her husband, Hank, and they flow together uniquely in prophetic demonstrations of the gifts of the spirit. Brenda is a published author with both Destiny Image and Charisma House. Brenda Kunneman's chapter in *The Force of Faith Decrees* was taken from her book, *Daily Decrees for Family Blessing and Breakthrough—Defeat the Assignments of Hell Against Your Family and Create Heavenly Atmospheres in Your Home.*

# Other Spirit-filled Books on Decrees

**The Daily Decree**
*Brenda Kunneman*

**The King's Decree**
*Jodie Hughes*

**Victory Decrees**
*Jennifer LeClaire*

**Turnaround Decrees**
*Jon & Jolene Hamill*

**Prayers & Decrees that Activate Angel Armies**
*Tim Sheets*

**Releasing Prophetic Solutions**
*Christy Johnston*

**Command Your Healing**
*Hakeem Collins*

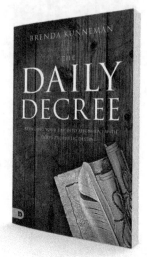